Playful Reading

Positive, Fun Ways to Build the Bond between Preschoolers, Books, and you

• Carolyn Munson-Benson •

Search INSTITUTE | Practical research benefiting children and youth

A Search Institute Publication

Playful Reading: Positive, Fun Ways to Build the Bond between Preschoolers, Books, and You

Carolyn Munson-Benson
Copyright © 2005 by Carolyn Munson-Benson

A Search Institute Publication

Search Institute® and Developmental Assets® are trademarks of Search Institute.

10 9 8 7 6 5 4 3 2
Printed on acid-free paper in the United States of America.

Search Institute
615 First Avenue Northeast, Suite 125
Minneapolis, MN 55413
612-376-8955 • 800-888-7828
www.search-institute.org

CREDITS
EDITORS: Rebecca Aldridge, Jennifer Griffin-Wiesner, Susan Wootten
BOOK DESIGN: Cathy Spengler Design
PRODUCTION COORDINATOR: Mary Ellen Buscher

LIBRARY OF CONGRESS CATALOGING-IN-PUBLICATION DATA
Munson-Benson, Carolyn.
  Playful reading : positive, fun ways to build the bond between preschoolers, books, and you / by Carolyn Munson-Benson.
     p. cm.
  Includes bibliographical references.
  ISBN 1-57482-857-6 (paperbook : alk. paper)
  1. Reading (Preschool)
  2. Reading—Parent participation.
  3. Children—Books and reading.
  I. Title.
LB1140.5.R4M86 2004
372.4—dc22

                    2004023379

ABOUT SEARCH INSTITUTE
Search Institute is an independent, nonprofit, nonsectarian organization whose mission is to provide leadership, knowledge, and resources to promote healthy children, youth, and communities. The institute collaborates with others to promote long-term organizational and cultural change that supports its mission. For a free information packet, call 800-888-7828.

For Liv and Kai,
my teachers

Contents

Introduction

In the beginning was relationship.

—Martin Buber

Building Relationships

· ·

THIS IS A BOOK ABOUT RELATIONSHIP—that of asset building and early
literacy, of people and books, of grown-ups and little ones. All are essential for young children's well-being and future success.

Developmental Assets are research-based "nutrients" that all children need. Every day, parents and significant others build these assets,
which are critical to healthy development, by honoring and implement-
ing proven ways to give each child a best chance to thrive, to flourish.

Playful Reading incorporates many such asset-building strategies.
It encourages adults to have fun and meaningful interactions with the
children they love by enjoying together acclaimed children's books.
In the process, those who care for and about preschoolers—teachers,
librarians, family members, adult friends, child-care providers—promote
the place of reading and the power of assets in young lives.

Those new to this framework may want to refer to the list of item-
ized Developmental Assets for preschoolers on pages 208–213. Others
may be content with the brief reminders that introduce every asset category at the beginning of each section of this book. In a nutshell, each
describes one of eight sets of Developmental Assets and its important
link to early literacy. The characters and stories featured in each section
reflect particular assets in action.

For each Developmental Asset category, you'll find:

* An introductory page;
* Five highlighted asset-rich titles;
* An overview of each featured title;
* Ways to promote talk about each book before and after a reading;
* Three suggested book-related activities, recipes, rituals, or
  reflections for each book; and
* A concluding bonus list of additional books that reflects a specific
  asset category.

A blueprint of the design of this activity book, in the chapter "More
about the World of Print and This Book" on page xiii, offers additional

insights about each component so you can make the most of read-aloud sessions.

As you dive into the books with a child, you may notice that some books highlight assets in more than one of the eight categories. A book such as *You Can Do It, Sam,* for example, featured in the "Empowerment" section, happens to illustrate other Developmental Asset categories, too, including Support, Constructive Use of Time, Commitment to Learning, and Social Competencies. Feel free to group such asset-rich examples with books in another section if it applies.

Keep 'Em Coming

Enjoy these books along with many others—beautiful ones, quirky ones, funny ones, familiar and favorite ones, award-winners and rewarding reads, concept books and books with beloved characters, rhyming texts, alphabet and counting books, series and sequels. Whether you feature the collection recommended here, asset category by asset category, as some preschool educators have done over the course of a year, or you simply include the titles along with other favorites when the spirit moves you, you'll be giving a gift of priceless value.

For one thing, you'll be promoting the read-aloud ritual—the single most important factor in raising readers. While most define literacy as the ability to read and write, early literacy is not about teaching young children *how* to decode the printed page. Instead, by reading aloud, the parent or primary caregiver, the preschool teacher, and the child-care provider support earlier stages that ready a young child for future success in school and in life. (Experts assert that to support readiness, adults need to supply children with 1,000 reading-related experiences before their first day of kindergarten.)

With assets in mind, book in hand, and a young child to keep you company, share this asset-rich literature and dive heart-first into activities that enhance all kinds of relationships. Bring each young child closer to what he or she is meant to be by using books to explore self, others, and the world. For these books and the linking activities, recipes, rituals, and reflections to have a meaningful impact, it's important to acknowledge the nature of some primary relationships:

    ✴ Adult to child;
    ✴ Adult to book;
    ✴ Child to book; and
    ✴ Book to world.

Adult to Child

Promoting early literacy and building Developmental Assets are *every-body's* business. Parents of preschoolers—particularly those ages 3 to 5—are an obvious audience for *Playful Reading*. But virtually anyone—a child-care provider, a preschool teacher, a librarian, a relative, a family literacy educator, a caregiver or a caring *giver*—has the power to enrich a young child's life.

A caring adult like you makes the difference. Without grown-ups to provide books that reflect assets, to initiate read-alouds, and to move from book to real-life action, nothing happens. When an adult opens the best books with a child, he or she opens both reader's and listener's eyes to an inner reality—an emotional landscape—and to a wider world. The very act of building a shared frame of reference, side by side, page after page, requires one-to-one attention, one-to-one *relating*.

Adult to Book

Unique read-aloud styles are appropriate for children at different stages of development. Tailor yours to your child's age and maturity level.

TERRIFIC FOR TODDLERS

If you are reading to an older toddler who uses at least 50 words in everyday speech, literacy experts recommend lots of exchanges between grown-up and child throughout a book. In other words, you encourage simple conversation. Preschoolers for whom English is a second language or who have spent little or no time with books will benefit initially from such a dialogue-packed read-aloud style.

Pausing every few pages during a reading provides chances to ask simple "what" questions of young listeners: "What's that? What is she doing? What is the bear holding? What color is the truck?" When a child answers with a correct word or two, the grown-up affirms the effort and expands upon the answer: "Yes, she's running . . . really fast." Or, "The bear is holding a birthday cake. That's right!" Make sure to supply answers whenever a child doesn't respond. If, for example, the child doesn't answer your question about a color, supply the answer. Then invite the listener to repeat the word, affirming this effort. For example, "Red! Great! It's a red fire truck!" As vocabulary grows over time, you can choose more open-ended questions.

PERFECT FOR PRESCHOOLERS

In contrast to the read-aloud approach with simple, frequent dialogue, for children around 4 years and older the best style underscores the importance of an entertaining romp from the beginning to the end of a book. Instead of a focus on managing behavior or asking questions that interrupt the flow of the story, move along, being expressive as you read. The success of this approach has less to do with an adult's talent for reading aloud—that is, her or his expressive skill—but rather how the grown-up interprets the nature of the event. When you get ready to read to a preschooler, you prepare to let loose. You get ready for fun.

Playful exploration still is important, however. Be sure to talk together about the story before and after a reading (for more information, see pages xiii–xv), unless there's a need to explain a confusing detail immediately. Just before revisiting a book you've read previously, encourage children to recall what happens, to talk about the meaning of new words they've encountered, to identify with or make sense of characters' actions, and to link the story to real life.

Child to Book

"Hello, book. I love you. I'm glad you're never very far away. You make me laugh. You make me wonder. You are a comfort. Here, let me hold you. Hello, book. "

This is the interior monologue I imagine when I see a toddler or preschooler connect with books. Ideally, this loyal and loving kinship to books begins as early as possible. Perhaps the little one has been in daily relationship with the written word since before birth, floating behind the mother's belly button, as Mama or another has read and sung to the awaited child.

Teachers and librarians report that it's usually easy to tell which preschoolers have had early experiences with books and which have not. For one thing, as Dorothy Butler, a renowned children's literature expert, has pointed out, it is the 3- and 4-year-olds who haven't had such exposure who are most likely to be destructive around books. For these children in particular, exposure to irresistible, age-appropriate books is crucial.

Book to World

In addition to providing a pleasant, simple activity for a set amount of time, a story may help child and adult make better sense of their world, expanding their understanding of ways to be. Through books, these explorers move into that wider world together. An ongoing encounter with beauty and language and a range of characters' lives ultimately shapes their own.

Playful Reading expands the definition of "activity book." While it features many active things to do with a child in a limited time frame, it also reveals proactive ways to be with a child in daily life. While it acknowledges the value of books as bridges to playful actions or extensions in the real world, it also honors the power of literature to change lives. It invites informed action to improve the world on behalf of your child, of all young children.

Onward and Upward

All that's left to do is to "dwell in possibility," meandering through these pages as you would a travel guide. With Developmental Assets in mind, book in hand, and a young child to keep you company, may your journey be as rewarding as the destination—happy engagement with words and the world.

More about the World of Print and This Book

The Big Picture

For each featured picture book, I offer a sketch of the plot and one or more of the characters, as well as the story's link to the Developmental Asset category in which it's featured. The book profiles can drive your decision making about which ones to borrow from the library (providing the best takeout in town!) now or later, and which are likely to appeal most to the child in your care.

Before You Read Together

On any first date that you arrange between book and child, the goal is to get things off to a great start. Perhaps you have skimmed the book yourself in order to add to the anticipation during introductions. In any case, you, as matchmaker, want to make the most of this first encounter with a specific book. Despite the old saying that "you can't tell a book by its cover," in the case of picture books, typically each does give tantalizing clues about what's to come. It's your calling to empower any child to recognize a good prospect when they see one.

The cover illustration as well as the endpaper design (found just inside the front and back covers) give clues. The title, which you can announce, does, too. Talk together about what you expect from the clues. Does this book promise laughs, adventure, engagement with a subject dear to this preschooler's heart? Does it prompt a recollection of a previous date with a similar book? With a sense of great satisfaction, a preschooler, eyeing the details, can predict what's going to happen, practice using words related to the story, and plunge ahead with greater curiosity. You, of course, can discover if it's a match made in heaven.

After You Read Aloud

Extended talk is the term used for the informal conversations that ideally precede and follow the sharing of a book. When my kids were preschoolers, we whizzed through piles of books in the course of any week. And while I don't recall shushing anybody who had a comment about a cover or who made a point about the invariably happy ending, I steered away from discussions that smacked of instruction. For the most part, I still do.

The pleasure principle—that books should be a source of positive and happy associations—is most important. Thus, I resist read-alouds where pleasure gives way to the need to preach. As a classroom teacher, I routinely checked students' comprehension, explored the meaning of new words and concepts, and encouraged young detectives to predict an unfamiliar book's content. At home, I shied away from such activities early on because I liked the freedom to focus solely on fun. I believed that the other stuff could wait.

But I was wrong about ignoring an essential piece of the read-aloud process—for preschoolers, in particular. I didn't appreciate at the time that reserving minutes for talk after reading a book together builds all-important *oral proficiency*. Don't let the fancy term fool you. Yes, the process is about building vocabulary long before a child must recognize and decode it on a page. Welcoming extended talk, however, is also an invitation to go exploring together, joyfully taking apart complicated words or ideas, delighting in word*play*, savoring language-rich conversations.

The operative word here is *exploration*. Since reading authorities prescribe rereading books any number of times, you do not need to do all of the exploring in one session. Together, you and your child can embark on a shared quest for meaning. Ideally, we grown-ups will listen more than we talk during these explorations as we empower children to try words on for size.

Word Banks

Kids who succeed at reading typically enter school with thousands of words they understand. Preschoolers sock these gems away for future use and draw upon them when they finally decode the printed page in school. Where do young children get these new words that they add to their mental word banks?

Many pop up repeatedly in conversations with an adult. Research shows that grown-ups are apt to use a core group of anywhere from 1,000 to 5,000 words in everyday exchanges, but experts recommend closer to 10,000 words by age 5 for eventual success at reading for meaning. Here's where children's books have the edge. Beyond that simple core of families' most often-used words, books hold twice as many as language spoken on prime-time TV or in conversations between college graduates. Unconsciously, young children go word-hunting for written language adults share with them, both during a read-aloud and, importantly, during extended talk before and after.

Whether you are a parent, child-care provider, preschool educator, or any other caregiver, make time for this extended talk. For each featured title in this book, you'll find suggestions for predicting what's in store (under the subhead "Before You Read Together") as well as more creative ways you can extend talk and playfully add to that word bank.

Literacy Links

Literacy links, or extensions, build bridges between story and world. The term *extensions,* used by literacy specialists, refers to anything that deepens understanding first gleaned from the pages of a book, then enriched through related action. Activities and recipes and rituals make stories come alive for children. They make it possible for a story to become more meaningful.

Literacy links also reveal the important place of print in our world—pointing to its many uses. They underscore the importance of being able to read in various aspects of life. For example, playing "store" incorporates:

* Food labels;
* Store signs and food coupons; and
* Special orders that require scribbling or pretend writing.

These items are *literacy props.* In fact, anything that promotes engagement with print qualifies—an alphabet puzzle, a poster with words, costumes or stick puppets for reenacting a particular story, and a flannel board or experience chart for recalling or repeating one. Props spur an emerging reader's awareness of words in print.

Some literacy links have multiple facets, but they can be simple, too. When you place magnetic alphabet letters on the fridge or write a love note dictated by the child to a loved one, you are making print part of everyday life.

Jumping and Jiving on the Road to Thriving

Jumping and jiving may not characterize all activities with preschoolers, but the phrase does underscore the role that delight plays in what you can do with them. Whenever possible, balance pleasurable, peaceful read-aloud times by following up with action-packed memory making.

Supporting a child at this stage is not about pulling workbook pages or flash cards out of a hat. There's nothing magical—or memorable— about forcing young children to do exercises or drills for which they're not developmentally ready. Faced with assessment mandates, teachers especially run the risk of creating curriculum that kills joy.

The relationship between book and asset-building action is a dance, with you and the preschooler in your life sashaying through days of real engagement with what jump-starts mind and body. Each book you read aloud, each project you savor, offers a chance to live in the moment and love the one you're with.

Helping young children to thrive, however, also requires honest reflection. One or more of the titles suggested in this book may prompt such soul-searching since they illustrate models of what healthy family life and preschool life can be. As you think about how you typically interact with your preschooler, if there's a disconnect between what can be and what is, take the opportunity to wonder why.

At this stage of life, young children are dependent on the big people to find them the "right" book at the right time. While there are topics that please lots of preschoolers, what engages one young child can be very different from what excites another. Responses can be dependent on who reads a selection aloud, even on the day or year a particular book comes their way. It's not only a good idea to indulge one child who is wild about dinosaurs or another who's mad about "Maisy" by sharing additional books about the preferred topic or character. It's also wise to expose every young child to multiple books about topics that have universal relevance, such as alphabet and counting books. Some experiences typical for preschoolers—like living through the sense of displacement that a newborn in the house can bring—also call for exposure to books that provide different perspectives and reassurance.

Ritual

The dictionary describes it as any practice or pattern of behavior regularly performed in a set manner. However, for young children there is nothing routine about ritual. Preschoolers are not apt to reject special rituals in the way that, at certain stages, they resist routines ranging from flushing to brushing. In fact, children more easily tolerate such responsibilities if they also participate in the *meaning* making and *memory* making of the rituals.

Take a mental inventory of the ones that already figure in your preschooler's experience—whether they're fairly common rituals, such as singing "Happy Birthday" around a cake aglow with candles, or they're more unique to your circumstances. Beginning new traditions when children are preschoolers and possess a heightened sense of wonder can be especially meaningful.

When I met Jan, she had her hands full, working part-time and caring for her three boys, all under 7. Her husband had been out of work for months. During a visit in their sparsely furnished living room, I noticed a low table covered with a simple pressed cloth. On the cloth, standing tall, covers out, like a colorful bouquet, was an array of picture books. At this point of focus in the room and around this source of inspiration, Jan had created rituals, bringing beauty and pleasure and laughter to her boys, even during a stressful period of family life.

Just as one puts fresh flowers in a vase, Jan made time for treks to the local library for fresh titles. Returning, she engaged her sons in another familiar ritual—together briefly admiring and gently arranging the new arrivals on this altar of sorts. She treated the books as if they were special, so her boys did, too. Each child knew he had access at any time to the bounty, but also could count on a daily read-aloud ritual to explore the world from a loving parent's lap. With simple observances, Jan put any number of assets into play, offering:

* An array of quality resources;
* Opportunities for her sons to offer help with simple chores that bring pleasure and order to their environment;
* Developmentally appropriate materials and experiences; and
* Language-rich activities, particularly being read to.

Jan also acted as a role model, showing the same kind of engagement with learning that she expected of and valued in her own young children. Building rituals into their lives and assets into their experience, she was willing and able to help them bloom.

Questions to Ask Yourself

. . . .

Ask yourself the following questions to help ensure that you're making reading with your preschooler playful and positive. You may also want to keep track for one week of the positive and negative messages you send to children in your life, specifically about their reading skills and habits, as well as their ways of being and behaving in general. In advance, brainstorm "positives" you can express (What a helper! I like your drawing! I knew you could do it!) and use them.

* How do I feel about my own reading habits and read-aloud skills? Am I self-conscious?
* How would others describe my attitude about reading and books?
* What, if anything, keeps me from reading to the child daily?
* How can I help shape the child's reading attitude and behavior through my actions?
* What, if anything, keeps me from offering easy access to terrific books at home?
* Do we make time for rhyme at our house?
* Do we make time to talk about a book, particularly before and after a reading?
* Do I usually choose only books that feature characters of the child's gender, so-called boy books or girl books?
* When's the last time we read a book that builds empathy with and appreciation for someone with a disability?
* Do we read books that include characters of many races and cultures?

Questions adapted from *Raising Kids Who Read* by Carolyn Munson-Benson, copyright © 2004 by YMCA Canada.

Daily Read-Aloud Chart

Use the following chart to keep track of how many minutes per day you spend reading with the child in your life.

SUN.	MON.	TUES.	WED.	THURS.	FRI.	SAT.	TOTAL MINUTES FOR THE WEEK

♥ Support

♥ *This Developmental Assets category focuses on family support, positive family communication, additional satisfying relationships with grown-ups, caring neighborhoods and other out-of-home settings, and parental involvement in and outside of the home. It plays an important part in describing healthy environments and promoting literacy for all children.*

• •

PARENTS AND PRIMARY CAREGIVERS are a young child's first and most important teachers. With heightened awareness from family, friends, and people in the wider community—the crucial other adult relationships—support for providing daily read-aloud time and access to a bounty of high-quality books for your preschooler is possible from every corner of the community. All young children need access to this bounty. Without it, they are not likely to regard books enthusiastically.

Offering a preschooler time to independently explore books is a worthy practice, but it's not enough. Equally important is the engaged presence of a caring grown-up, such as you, who gradually extends read-aloud sessions as a preschooler's attention span grows. This engagement includes introducing a wide range of books, frequent reading, and stimulating follow-up conversations.

Molly Goes Shopping

· ·

by Eva Eriksson, translated by Elisabeth Kallick Dyssegaard. New York:
R & S Books, 2003.

IT WON'T GO UNNOTICED that the main character in this book is a pig
whose grandma appears to be a polar bear. What's more, the pig is sent
on errands that would be daunting for most preschoolers. In the event
your child pleads with you to let her or him venture out alone to the
supermarket, keep your wits about you and note that (1) pigs are more
mature for their age, (2) this plucky porker is probably at least 6 years
old, and/or (3) the story is, after all, just make-believe, with big doses
of whimsy characteristic of this Swedish author's other tales. Then prepare to marvel at the wise ways of Grandma, who dotes on Molly (who
"has gotten so smart lately") and consistently supports her through the
trials and errors that are part of growing up. This charming tale illustrates the crucial elements of family support, not to mention positive
family communication.

Before You Read Together

Explore the details of the cover illustration with the child. Can he or
she figure out where this pig has shopped, what she may have pur-
chased, how she'll manage getting home, and whether she might be
the Molly in the title? Invite your young companion(s) to identify the
foods in the picture.

After You Read Aloud

- After savoring the story, you may want to return to pages that
  show Molly's facial expressions and together guess the feelings
  they reveal: when is she proud, shy, embarrassed, surprised,
  angry, sad, worried, scared, sorry, confused, happy?

- Play with the concept of opposites, noting parts of the story that illustrate or suggest: lost/found, heavy/light, happy/sad, old/ young, fast/slow, big/little, hello/good-bye, remember/forget, true/false, over/under, beginning/end. Brainstorm other opposites together.

Play Store

The pretend store uses lots of literacy props—play items that feature different kinds of printed words as well as opportunities to play at simple writing and counting. These props are usually easy to assemble.

In a plastic storage container or a double-strength paper or canvas shopping bag, store an assortment of clean, empty boxes and cans that boast familiar logos and combinations of alphabet letters (Jell-O pudding, Cheerios, Campbell's soup, Uncle Ben's rice, etc.). When opening cans to be saved, remove the bottom end and be sure the rim has no jagged, sharp edges. Add to these items:

- ☐ Play cash register or cash box
- ☐ Toy phone
- ☐ Play money
- ☐ Clipped coupons
- ☐ Pencil and paper
- ☐ Small- and medium-size paper bags

Once you've enjoyed repeat encounters with *Molly Goes Shopping*, tie up an empty bakery box with string, pop a few potatoes in a cloth bag, add a coin purse, and encourage dramatic reenactment of the tale. Without lots of prompts from you, observe how the child interprets the familiar story.

For a more involved activity, create some signs for the young grocer: Checkout, On Sale, CLOSED, OPEN, Only $1. Let the storekeeper stack and sort goods on makeshift shelves, chairs, or planks. Add labels to designate the sections or shelves in the store: Meats, Soups, Produce. (Incorporating such print reminds the prereader of its usefulness in the real world.) Invite the preschooler to cut out magazine pictures of foods to jazz up these signs. (Laminating them at a copy shop guarantees a longer shelf life.) Pretend to phone in orders for the grocer to jot down and fill. Ask about suggested best buys.

Practice Makes Perfect

I have a vivid memory of my mother watching from an apartment window as I, at 5 or 6, make a solo trip across a city street to mail two letters I've printed and drawn for cousins far away. As I stand on that corner, my heart is full.

I am just like the grown-ups, out there alone, careful to cross on the green light, about to send my own creations out into the world. I can still recall the stretch to reach the mailbox handle and then, in a blur of shouts and bodies, several big boys yank the envelopes from my hand and run away down the street. What sudden desolation I feel, even as my mother quickly joins me on the street corner, and especially when we find the torn and crumpled remains halfway down the block. The boys, failing to find any money inside, are long gone.

Perhaps this is why *Molly Goes Shopping* strikes such a sympathetic chord in me. The young child's eagerness to be of use, to venture out into the world, to try something new that the big kids or big people do, is offset by a reality that doesn't always match what's envisioned.

Children face disappointments. They disappoint themselves and, at times, their elders. "It can happen to anyone," Grandma tells Molly, despite the fact that Molly's lie faulting the store clerk has outraged Grandma and prompted her trip to the store to give the innocent clerk a piece of her mind. She sees Molly for what she is—a child trying out solutions, afraid of disappointing, unsure of why she has lied. Gently and firmly, Grandma informs her that she must not lie anymore. She honors Molly with yet another responsibility, but soon Molly faces another crisis, which for some adults may be reason enough to withhold support. Grandma, however, kindly helps Molly find the "stolen" purse, and again entrusts her with it. Grandma's intent, clearly, is to see the child she loves succeed.

Recall your responses when you've made mistakes. Now think about how your child would say you handled her or his own failure—the time he or she broke a glass, told a fib, wet the bed, wailed in the movie theater, ruined a new pair of shoes. As hard as we may try, we may not always react perfectly. When a child disappoints us, makes a big mistake, or fails to deliver, we may at times be quick to judge or blame. Recollect your words and reactions the time a child in your care said a bad word, scribbled in a book, or slapped another child. Have you ever regretted saying or doing something to a young child, but neglected later to say "I'm sorry"? In a quiet time, a milk-and-cookies time, a you-and-me time, spend five minutes telling:

* About a mistake you made, yesterday or when you were 4.
* How everybody makes mistakes sometimes, how practice makes perfect, how next time one can always try to do better, how you still love someone even when he or she makes a mistake.
* Why you're sorry you were so angry or mean or distant that time when . . .

Welcome and listen to the child's feelings about what you've shared. Listen and love that child, no matter what.

Job Jar

Think about the ways a preschooler is already able to be a helper. On strips of paper, print simple jobs that young children may be able to manage on their own. (If you wish, include a symbol or sketch of the task.) Examples include directives to match and sort socks, put away toys, clear the table, sweep (with a child-size broom), or line up shoes. Ask your child to add some suggestions. Put these strips of paper in a jar. While you are cleaning, when the child asks to be of use, or at specified times each week, let the young helper choose one strip and have you read the instruction. Supply the necessary equipment to complete the project.

You may need to give step-by-step guidance the first few times that he or she does a task. Some jobs may be beyond your little helper's present capabilities, so have an alternative ready in case the child becomes frustrated. Look for what goes well. Praise best efforts and give thanks for completed jobs.

A Birthday for Frances

by Russell Hoban, illustrated by Lillian Hoban. New York: HarperCollins, 1995.

AS IN HIS OTHER FRANCES BOOKS, which are deservedly classics, author Russell Hoban perfectly captures here the mind-set of a young child dealing with challenges and feelings common to this age group. The characters, a family of badgers, represent "ourselves-in-fur" and not only mirror human family dynamics but model caring responses by the grown-ups. The badger parents clearly recognize that a young one's expression of negative words and acts, while unwelcome, are also understandable at this age and stage. Frances, like most preschoolers, wants it to be *her* birthday, and she wrestles with the dilemma of giving her sister a gift she'd just as soon keep herself. With the loving support of her parents, Frances finally chooses one. Woven through the text are examples of asset-rich family life, with the grown-ups providing high levels of love, attention, and nurturing in a way responsive to a child's individuality.

Before You Read Together

Can your preschooler name the cover's illustrated clues that show what the story will be about? The title says *A Birthday for Frances,* but the name on the cake says "Gloria." Ask your child what this could mean. Find out if the child is curious about the kind of animals—badgers—depicted.

After You Read Aloud

- Here's an opportunity to find out about favorites: ask the child to tell you about her favorite present ever, the best part of a birthday party, whom he'd invite to his next party, a favorite food or cake, the best party she remembers.

- Frances likes to pretend to spell out words. Rather than correcting or teasing her, her parents play along and respond in a matter-of-fact manner to these early attempts to honor the power of print. Ask your child: Is there a word or words you would like to see in print? Can you recognize letters in your own name yet?
- Suggest that the two of you make up a simple song, perhaps only two to four rhyming lines, just as Frances does, about something important. Print it or tape-record it.

Parties for the Preschool Set

Is there anything as wonderful or potentially wearying as children's birthday parties? Many parents hold a first-year party, comprised of grown-up friends or family, when they're as likely to be celebrating surviving Baby's bouts of colic or crack-of-dawn feedings. Then they graduate to a toddler-style party with at least one adult per child, and eventually to the bona fide birthday bash.

Now, at 3 years of age, partygoers range from very fragile to the wild and easily excitable. Each is on the verge of awareness that a party is something special. However, these children are not yet ready to sustain interest in any one activity or, for that matter, in their young host—the supposed center of attention. By age 4, children typically love party-giving and party-going. However, their boundless energy and appetite for the unique and new pose party-planning challenges as well. Developmental experts and party veterans alike warn that 5-year-olds can be more critical and conservative—with a show-me attitude and a need to protect their turf.

A birthday party is no time for moral lessons about sharing or shoving. The birthday star and the guests benefit from the supportive presence of a primary caregiver plus two to three other adults. These reinforcements along with the following party how-tos help keep things running smoothly.

* Theme parties not only make decisions easier regarding favors, cake decoration, and activities but also can reflect (and affirm) a young child's current interest. Feature a favorite book character, perhaps with a garden theme inspired by *The Tale of Peter Rabbit* or some monkey business with *Curious George*.

* As a rule of thumb, keep the total number of young guests
  to one more than the child's age.
* The party shouldn't last beyond 1½ hours.
* Smooth the transition as guests arrive by providing access
  to toys or to blank or theme-related placemats to color.
* To honor short attention spans, keep things moving.
* Use tried-and-true group activities. Some ideas include playing
  rhythm instruments; marching; hearing an engaging read-aloud
  linked to the party's theme; playing noncompetitive, simple games
  such as Duck, Duck, Goose; trying on costumes; participating in
  simple treasure hunts; and unwrapping favors.
* Keep in mind that simple food is best: cake and ice cream, small
  sandwiches, carrot and celery sticks.
* Most preschoolers wish it were their party (or even pretend it is).
  Keep each guest happy with a series of inexpensive surprises—
  a wrapped trinket after gift opening, a treat bag of munchies,
  a balloon at party's end.

Gift Giving

Siblings' birthdays present the opportunity to school the youngest in
the ultimate satisfactions of giving rather than getting. The chance to
choose a gift for another can be empowering. And a trip to find the gift
also offers the opportunity for adult and child to spend one-on-one
time together.

Edible play dough is an example of a homemade gift alternative
that any caring adult can help a child make. Roll out and cut the dough
into heart shapes or gingerbread figures before the grown-up bakes
and both of you wrap the item.

GINGERBREAD PLAY DOUGH

1/2 cup oil

1 teaspoon cinnamon

3 tablespoons corn syrup

2 1/2 cups flour

1/2 cup sugar

1 teaspoon baking soda

1 teaspoon ground ginger

1/2 teaspoon salt

Water

(continued on next page)

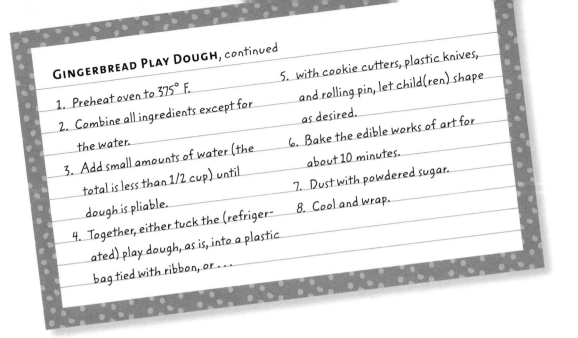

GINGERBREAD PLAY DOUGH, continued

1. Preheat oven to 375° F.

2. Combine all ingredients except for the water.

3. Add small amounts of water (the total is less than 1/2 cup) until dough is pliable.

4. Together, either tuck the (refrigerated) play dough, as is, into a plastic bag tied with ribbon, or . . .

5. with cookie cutters, plastic knives, and rolling pin, let child(ren) shape as desired.

6. Bake the edible works of art for about 10 minutes.

7. Dust with powdered sugar.

8. Cool and wrap.

A Birthday Ritual

Initiate a project inspired by Debra Frasier's book *On the Day You Were Born* by creating a time capsule to tuck away until your preschooler's 18th or 21st birthday celebration.

Typically, family members, neighbors, and friends in a child's life provide items for the keepsake—loving notes describing what they value about the child, favorite times spent together, memories of the birth, or other milestones in the first years. A relative may want to tuck in a valued possession he or she wishes to pass on. Siblings and young friends can contribute special drawings and dictated messages.

Photocopy several pages of photos of your growing child in action. Include pictures of the child's bedroom, favorite toys, a pet, and special friends and adults. Draw an outline of his hands that he can color. Interview her on an audiotape.

You may wish to copy the front page of a newspaper from the day of the child's birth, and list on separate stationery the names of popular songs and shows, famous people, current trends, and important events to place inside along with the headlines.

Consider holding a ceremony prior to storing the collected mementos. For example, read aloud *On the Day You Were Born.* Then place everything in a mildew-resistant container and label it. Make sure two or more people know where the time capsule is stored so that someone remembers where to find it in order to present it when the child is grown.

A time-honored and popular variant of this celebration is the "Child of the Week" preschool tradition. Each child takes a turn as the "star" who, with the help of family members, mounts and displays personal items such as photos, baby clothes, favorite possessions, and drawings to tell about at special times during a week.

Adam's Daycare

. . . .

by Julie Ovenell-Carter, illustrated by Ruth Ohi. Toronto: Annick Press, 1997.

REFLECTING A SITUATION familiar to a majority of young children, this story features three preschoolers and a baby in the able and loving care of Ina, the child-care provider. It's a story that sets a standard for parents who want the best for their children when they must be away. It invites comparisons by young children exposed (or not) to components such as dramatic playtime, an art activity, a trip to the mailbox, a mishap, an affirmation, exploration in the garden, snack time, story time, and retrieval by their parents. Ina is nurturing and accepting. She provides stability and security, as the Developmental Assets framework recommends, and she and the young children's parents share a consistent and understanding approach.

Before You Read Together

A friendly-looking grown-up, with a baby in a backpack, lifts a boy— is it Adam?—up to the slot to mail a letter, while two other preschoolers examine flora and fauna nearby. A dog and a cat appear to be along for the walk. Ask your listener if she thinks the woman on the cover is a mother to all of the children pictured, despite the word *daycare* in the title. Her own experiences will inform the predictions.

Your child may spend time in a facility with access only to an attached playground. If so, ask your child what he thinks about this neighborhood setting? Does this first peek at what's to come in the book inspire immediate comparisons to the child's own care situation? As you read, challenge her to look for things that are the same and things that are different about Adam's daycare and her own daytime setting.

After You Read Aloud

- Ask your child to identify which child of the foursome doesn't go home at the end of the day. Ask her if she thinks this could be Ina's own baby.
- The characters reflect different emotions. Discuss the feelings shown when a child waves good-bye to an exiting parent, when a small accident occurs, when one receives praise, and when something goes wrong. Talk together about emotions that the child feels related to time spent in an out-of-home setting. Ask: "What makes you happy (sad, mad) when you are there?"

Child-Care Choices

Books often model better ways to be and move us to action. If you are a parent, do you find many similarities as you compare the environment in the story with that of your child's provider or preschool? If you are a provider or an educator, does the book's setting prompt you to think anew about important elements to add or improve? A stimulating and supportive environment influences brain development, positive identity, and future success. Jackie Johnston, a licensed early childhood family education specialist for more than two decades, provides seven pointers for assessing an early childhood setting. Ask yourself if your child's setting or your site reflects the following:

1. Is the child-care setting a safe learning environment for young children? The most important consideration should be safety.
2. Is the environment nurturing? Does the provider treat the children with respect and caring, demonstrating a knowledge of child development and realistic expectations?
3. Does the provider or teacher interact often with the children, offering them ongoing opportunities for dialogue? Is the language of high quality?
4. Does the grown-up use appropriate, positive talk as well as a variety of words and explanations, regardless of the children's ages? Does the caregiver affirm each child?
5. Maria Montessori, M.D., wrote, "Play is the work of the child." Is there a range of activities and playthings? Are there high-quality books and ways for children to extend the stories into their play?

6. Do the preschoolers have opportunities for exposure to outside resources—field trips or guest visitors? (Many community resources are available to centers and home sites.)

7. Do parents have opportunities to grow and learn as well? A truly high-quality program will provide information on specific issues such as separation anxiety as well as the latest research findings. The provider spends time talking with parents, even journaling about the child's day. This practice of communicating and learning as a family unites the grown-ups in a common goal, and parents talking about the day with the child sets a pattern for daily sharing that can be carried on for years.

Portable Post Office

Ideally, after their leisurely walk to the nearest mailbox, any of these preschoolers could make a beeline for a "writing center" at Ina's house. A staple in any preschool classroom or child-care setting, it's a table or learning center with materials for producing the primitive scribbles that eventually mimic alphabet letters, particularly the ones in a child's name. Provide at-home opportunities as well to experiment freely with the following supplies:

- ☐ Paper in varied sizes and colors
- ☐ Pens and pencils
- ☐ Envelopes
- ☐ Safety scissors
- ☐ Glue stick
- ☐ Stamp pad and several stamps, such as a date stamp or picture stamp
- ☐ Colored markers and crayons
- ☐ Stickers
- ☐ Small pencil sharpener

Add inexpensive postage stamps and a bundle of unopened junk mail, brochures, and flyers to convert the writing center into a pretend post office. A 9-by-12-inch cake pan with a sliding lid can easily become a portable post office. The child can carry supplies from one writing surface to another or take the kit on trips beyond home.

To further underscore this use of the alphabet, you can point out features of mail, like the address on the envelope and different kinds of stamps. At the post office, invite your child to pick out a few current stamps to save and savor. Occasionally send little ones a picture post-card or a simple "I love you" greeting, as most children thrill to receive mail. The caregiver or teacher can encourage preschoolers to mail a drawing or dictated message to VIPs in their lives.

Turning Off and Tuning In

In *Touchpoints Three to Six,* authors T. Berry Brazelton, M.D., and Joshua D. Sparrow, M.D., make the case that children feel parents' stress. They sense when parents remain "on call" even when they are home, dividing attention between work and children. In an era when 9-to-5 boundaries are disappearing, Drs. Brazelton and Sparrow strongly encourage parents and caregivers to use certain practices, such as:

* Reserving specific time every day to be wholly present for your child;
* Making a daily habit of "just hanging out" and enjoying "floor time" when the child knows that "you are his"; and
* Periodically rethinking your priorities and assessing the effects on your children of your current choices.

The parents in *Adam's Daycare* honor these practices. Anna's mom takes the time to admire her child's potful of dandelions and departs wearing some in her hair. Molly's daddy waits patiently while she finishes her popcorn and, carrying her on his shoulders, sports a small crown as they head for home. Adam's mother embraces him as if he were a little baby monkey. Surely these parents have many responsibilities and not enough time in which to fulfill them. Yet, each focuses on that primary responsibility, awaiting their return.

TRANSITIONS

Here are some helpful hints for transitioning from work to home in order to give children what they need at this potentially stressful time of day:

* Turn away from the world of work by shutting off electronic links to it, such as the cell phone, beeper, fax, Internet, and e-mail.
* Guarantee the awaiting child one-to-one attention with talk about each other's experiences during the day, as well as loving, reassuring, reconnecting touch.
* Don't use television as a babysitter.
* Create a transitional ritual (such as reading a book together) that the child can count on and for which the tired adult learns to save up energy, especially since most children will be weary once they return home from daycare or preschool.

Somebody Loves You, Mr. Hatch

· ·

by Eileen Spinelli, illustrated by Paul Yalowitz. New York: Simon & Schuster, 1991.

SOLITARY AND SOBER MR. HATCH is in a rut until, one Valentine's Day, the mail carrier delivers a gigantic heart-shaped box of chocolates and this message from a secret admirer: "Somebody loves you." One simple affirmation creates an amazing change. Mr. Hatch, wondering who loves him, starts sharing, talking, and supporting his neighbors in heart-warming ways, until he discovers that the gift and message have been delivered to the wrong address. In fact, when the mix-up prompts him to return to his old way of life, the neighbors notice and make sure that Mr. Hatch understands that somebody loves him, after all, an example of asset 4—caring neighbors.

Before You Read Together

A peek at the cover shows Mr. Hatch popping out of a heart-shaped opening surrounded by ribbon, as if he were a gift. What does your child guess about his personality from the posture (arms open wide) and facial expression of this cartoonlike character?

After You Read Aloud

- You may want to list all the "somebodies" who love the pre-schooler. Ask: "Whom do you love?"
- Discover what symbols, activities, and feelings the child already associates with Valentine's Day.

Out and About

Ask me to name the standout moments in my children's lives, *particularly* when they were preschool age, and I'd probably cite a handful of seasonal neighborhood rituals. Our extended family was tight-knit but lived far away from one another. Relatives were hard to top on holidays or special visits, but they were too many miles distant for regular interactions. We benefited, fortunately, from a band of parents and children within sight of our driveway, open to celebrations that fostered intergenerational connections.

Spontaneity ruled. Nobody sweated the details. And it took only one or two people to ignite a spark of interest in others. Is there somebody on your street waiting to join you in expanding children's circle of caring grown-ups? Could you provide the spark? Would these or similar seasonal rituals make life richer for your child? For you?

* One year, a mom crazy about the Fourth of July pranced down our avenue with her three little boys and their dad, waving flags and playing a pretend fife and drums. Several families joined the ragtag band and a tradition was born. Starting in the family's backyard, where patriotic tunes blared from a boom box, our motley crew paraded a mere one and a half street lengths. We pulled toddlers and patriotic paraphernalia in decorated Red Flyers. Some of us donned hastily concocted costumes; a Statue of Liberty with torch and green bedsheet was one. We didn't draw crowds, though some on their porch steps approved of the spectacle with grins and cheers. There were no entry requirements, no judges—just lemonade and laughter at the end of a giddy march.

* Most years in Minnesota, we can count on one or two "snow days," when a storm dumps enough flakes to halt business as usual. For a couple of years, two families down the block used to appear about midday outside for a trek. Snowsuited tykes and sleds in tow, we joined them and trudged to a pizza parlor that rarely closed. As we made our way through a silent and serene winter fairyland, not a moving car in sight, toward lunch and shared silliness, kids and grown-ups alike experienced a sense of high adventure.

* Each Halloween the young family on the corner welcomed munchkins and parents back to their house once the trick-or-treating was over. Some of the grown-ups came in costume, too. One year the little ones bobbed for apples and we all sipped cider. But the point was to get a longer look at our favorite ghosts and goblins while we enjoyed each other's company.

* In another neighborhood, each spring a dad with daughters many miles away invited our son and a friend to comb the lane for a winter's worth of litter, providing a chance to serve and a reason to connect.

* The Saturday before Mother's Day, two of us, with grown children, invited a handful of preschoolers to decorate prebaked cookies in one of our kitchens. We wrapped the finished colorful creations in cellophane and ribbon and attached love-you notes. Later their moms admitted that the gift of some quiet time on a Saturday morning was as welcome a present as the sweets the next day. We, on the other hand, had relished the chance to spend some time with young children again.

Love Offerings

With Mr. Hatch's neighbors as inspiration, send a handmade valentine—SOMEBODY LIKES YOU!—anytime of the year. Involve the child in befriending one or two neighbors in particular—the widow who has lived on your street for years, for example, or the young couple who just moved onto the block.

Delivery of a "May basket" to someone's door on the first of May is a custom observed around the United States. The gift comes anonymously, typically in the form of a small basket or cone-shaped container filled with treats such as raisins, almonds, and candy. On two occasions, on our doorstep I've found one left by a child. This seasonal sign of friendship never fails to warm my heart. I still have the handmade woven paper basket once filled with delectable homemade sweets, made by a neighborhood kindergartner, now a grown artist.

On a recent May Day, I found a construction paper cone attached to a wobbly pipe cleaner hanging from our doorknob. Two sprites had rung our bell and run. I couldn't help laughing over the contents—leftover foil-wrapped Easter eggs, some pennies, and several blades of grass (always welcome after our long winters). I gave thanks for preschoolers in our midst.

Help a preschooler forge a friendship with the recipient of his art-work or friendly messages: "We like your garden." "You have a pretty cat." "Thanks for always saying 'Hi!'" Let repeated readings about Mr. Hatch and his neighbors teach her about the transformative power of simple gestures of friendship, and that kindness is likely to be reciprocated.

Getting to Know You

The editor of a metropolitan magazine once asked me and a few others to each praise our own neighborhood's best features in an issue. Nearby access to coffee shops and hardware stores, proximity to parks, and area architecture or history were among the facets worthy of focus when the profiles appeared. The editor in chief ruefully observed in his column that only two of us had mentioned the existence of friendly neighbors.

Just as parents, caregivers, and teachers communicate with each other in a child-care or preschool setting via newsletters, informal con-versations, and meetings, neighbors benefit from getting to know each other as well. A common bit of advice to asset builders is, at the very least, to know by name the children and youth on one's street. If organ-izing an annual block party seems too ambitious a project, consider going door-to-door with your preschooler to collect from willing contributors the names of all family members, addresses, and home phone. As you go, together come up with symbols to associate with specific neighbors—for example, Joe Jackson's red door, Rosalba's ferns in the shade garden, the Jenningses' cat Fred. Make copies of your list, adding symbols to your own sheet for fun. Deliver copies to your neighbors. In an emer-gency or simply when needing a reminder of a neighbor's name, the informal directory provides the info. Creating a list of names and phone numbers of children and families in a preschool classroom or child-care setting builds community, too.

The Key to My Heart

. . . .

by Nira Harel, illustrated by Yossi Abulafia. La Jolla, CA: Kane/Miller Publishers, 2003.

LOCKED OUT OF THE HOUSE, Jonathan and his father retrace the dad's steps. While seeking the lost keys and cherished key chain, the boy interacts with those who embody assets linked to other adult relationships—generous and helpful grown-ups at businesses that they visit. Once they recover the lost item in an unlikely place, Jonathan's dad affirms why the picture of his child, on the ring, is the most important "key" of all—the key to identifying to whom the ring belongs and, even more significantly, the key to his heart.

Before You Read Together

The front cover shows a key ring with various keys and an attached leather-framed picture of a little boy. The back reveals that same boy twirling the key ring. Ask your child questions such as the following: Whose keys are these? The boy's? Someone else's? And what do the words "the key to my heart" mean? Can such a key be seen, or is it invisible? What does such a key open?

After You Read Aloud

- Talk about the places that you regularly visit, such as the post office, grocery store, bank, or library. Ask the child if she has a favorite or two. Talk about what helpful people or features make these places worthy of a visit.
- Like the dad in the story, identify what the keys on your key chain open. Invite the preschooler to recall and identify their uses as Jonathan did: "This is the key to . . ."

Photo Op

Keys fascinate many preschoolers. The power to unlock doors can be symbolic of the power to unlock the mysteries and unknowns in the child's life. Recreate the character's prized possession by producing a photo attachment for either your own key ring or a set of keys to pretend locks for your preschooler to claim. Or make both!

Your child can help you make a framed photo to serve as the key ring's most important feature. If making an attachment for your own key ring, find a wallet-size photo or cut an image from a larger snapshot of your child(ren). For the child's key ring, select a picture the preschooler desires—of you, the family pet, or any cherished item. You'll need:

- ☐ Patterned paper, such as gift wrap
- ☐ Photo
- ☐ Two glasses or jar lids (about ½ inch difference in diameter) or a compass for drawing circles
- ☐ Sheet of double-thick laminate and a laminator (available at many copy stores)
- ☐ Scissors
- ☐ Glue stick
- ☐ Hole punch

With a pencil, draw circles of one size around the chosen photo and the patterned paper. Leave at least ½ inch more around the portion of the photo to be visible. Cut around these shapes. Use a glass or another guide approximately ½ inch smaller to center and draw a second circle within the paper's larger circle. Cut out the inner circle.

Apply glue to the backside of the paper ring and carefully affix it to the photo as a frame. At a photocopying store, laminate (with double-thick stock) your creation and cut again around the outer circle. Punch a hole into the top of the laminate frame. Attach the key ring.

For the child's use, you can donate keys that no longer have a purpose or buy a few inexpensive ones in varying sizes and colors at the local hardware store. You can also get a simple metal ring on which to put the keys. Add the photo attachment.

Neighborhood Map or Vehicle Mat

Introduce the preschooler to simple mapmaking by creating a map of the neighborhood on a paper mat. Or if you are in an area near a number of businesses, include a two- to three-block area of places you often pass or visit. You don't need to include every structure, of course—only those that have significance for the child. And don't worry about your drawing skills: preschoolers are just beginning to understand the one-to-one correspondence of real locations and the symbols that represent them.

Involve the preschooler in the process. Use whatever suits your purposes for the background—a length of butcher paper or a light solid color from a gift wrap roll. For a paper mat, over which the preschooler will be rolling toy vehicles, you can affix a cardboard base to make it more durable.

Draw approximate lengths and locations of streets as well as familiar landmarks. If you are creating a mat on which small toy cars and other vehicles can be rolled, use one of these cars to gauge the coordinating size of streets, driveways, and parking lots.

On an outing together, snap pictures of the fronts of chosen buildings or homes. Then once they are developed, affix them to spots on the map where the structures are found. (The child can use crayons or markers instead, adding colors to predrawn outlines with the shapes and colors of the buildings.) Take pictures of the vehicle(s) that transport you to these places and pictures of you and your neighbors. Cutouts of the vehicles and people, with the snapshot backs glued to popsicle sticks, become stick puppets that can interact with each other and visit familiar haunts. If you wish to extend the life of the finished product once the creation is complete, laminate the map or mat on equipment that can handle a very large format (available at copy stores). Then trim the four sides.

You may prefer to create a make-believe town. However, replicating the child's familiar world creates unique opportunities for dramatic play, with children revealing their take on real-life situations. Using props that mirror their world, they can practice for future interactions. And older preschoolers can compare their creation to actual large-scale maps of the same area.

Simple Gifts

I was standing on a city street corner with my daughter, waiting for the light to turn green. From the floral shop behind us, a man in an apron appeared and offered my three-year-old one perfect long-stemmed rose. She looked with wonder at the unexpected gift as he explained that her smile, seen from inside the shop, had warmed his heart. The man then turned to me and said, "If it's okay with your mother."

I nodded. We both said "thank you" and proceeded across the street. I walked. She levitated, or so it seemed; the act of kindness had a magical effect on her. Had she ever before looked closely at the petals of a rose? Had she ever known the bloom could be so soft, each petal curled around the next? And the scent! This new sensory delight was a beautiful benchmark in her personal history. What a gift it was, coming as it did from out of the blue, but also from someone who represented a larger community of others whom she affected—with something as simple as a smile—and who affected her.

Yes, I know, there is plenty of reason to protect the youngest against potential predators. We need to be clear about urging children to accept gifts from strangers only when in our company. We need to be observant about all who initiate conversations and aware of procedures that help young children to distinguish between good and bad touch, that empower them to tell others if they feel afraid or ashamed or sad about a past or continuing form of contact.

But I resist the inclination to be so protective that there is no place for a stranger's token of friendship. In the interest of instilling in my preschooler an awareness of people who are good-hearted and, in time of trouble, can be sources of support, I was thankful for that rose. It signaled for both of us that warmth and kindness are a part of the wider world. Following are some ways you can extend this warmth and kindness:

* At your workplace or in your neighborhood, offer young children cheerful hellos, a listening ear, an eye-to-eye greeting, an affirmation, an unexpected helping hand.
* Gently encourage your preschooler to say "thank you" and remember to praise him later for remembering to express thanks.
* Supply the names of familiar coworkers, clerks, and public servants to her and model the habit of offering friendly greetings.
* Add fun to errands or excursions in your neighborhood when the child is along.
* Give an unexpected gift to a known or needy child in the coming week.

Support Bonus Best Bets

- **dear juno** by Soyung Pak, illustrated by Susan Kathleen Hartung. New York: Viking, 1999.

- **It Takes a Village** by Jane Cowan-Fletcher. New York: Scholastic, 1994.

- **Lilly's Purple Plastic Purse** by Kevin Henkes. New York: Greenwillow Books, 1996.

- **Old MacDonald** by Amy Schwartz. New York: Scholastic, 1999.

- **On Mother's Lap** by Ann Herbert Scott, illustrated by Glo Coalson. New York: McGraw-Hill, 1972.

- **The Sick Day** by Patricia MacLachlan, illustrated by Jane Dyer. New York: Random House Children's Books, 2001.

- **The Story of Little Babaji** by Helen Bannerman, illustrated by Fred Marcellino. New York: HarperCollins, 1996.

Empowerment

Actions speak louder than words: the way grown-ups make time for children, the way they create a safe and enriching environment, the way they seek out and celebrate the good in children's early imperfect efforts reveals that they truly value the young. Even young children can offer service to others and be given useful roles. Rather than solely being acted upon, they can make choices and assign value to what they do in their everyday experiences.

• •

SOME PEOPLE VIEW READING as a peripheral pastime—an enjoyable but irrelevant activity for preschoolers. These people deserve to know the critical part that early and daily exposure to books and read-aloud time plays in children's future success. They need to know that making time for daily reading is one of the most important ways they can serve the children they cherish.

Research shows the amazing potency of messages from parents and other caring adults. Preschoolers who regularly receive daily positive feedback are much more likely to achieve later in school. In contrast, those who hear so-called prohibitions from an early age are more likely to struggle. Daily criticism, however good-natured or culturally acceptable, instills in children a "can't do" self-concept.

In a landmark study reported in *Meaningful Differences in the Everyday Experience of Young American Children* by Betty Hart and Todd R. Risley, Baltimore, P.H. Brooks, 1993, the researchers found that children in welfare and working-class families receive many more discouraging remarks than their peers in professional families. If the attempt is to "toughen up" a child for the real world, as one authority who highlights differences between socioeconomic classes once suggested to me, the result is not what's intended. Frequent positive feedback gives young children confidence and motivation. Gentle guidance and responsiveness empower. Offering reading or book-related affirmations lays the groundwork for later accomplishment. Informed adults need to alter behavior to secure a better future for their children. Otherwise, the beginning reader is not likely to measure up.

Guided discovery is a practice that prompts affirmations. You show, step by step, how best to handle reading and writing materials and then take note of the times that the child follows suit. Such noticing encourages positive behaviors. For example, look for chances to comment on the behaviors of a child who chooses to look at books, handles them with care, and "reads" to or with a sibling. Affirm the child for listening intently, asking questions before and after a story, and putting books away.

Edward in Deep Water

· ·

by Rosemary Wells. New York: Dial Books for Young Readers, 1995.

This story, one in the Edward the Unready series by premier author and illustrator Rosemary Wells, hinges on Edward's parents' reassuring proclamation: "Not everyone is ready for the same things at the same time." Edward's misgivings about going to a pool party are evident: he wears his water wings while his mother wraps a birthday present, even after his parents suggest that he leave them at home, since the previous summer he'd swum without them. His worst fears are realized at the event when two playmates remove the wings and stricken Edward goes under.

The rescue by the lifeguard and the group hug by worried grown-ups and peers illustrate assets in action: Adults reassure young children that their safety and well-being are a high priority, and that they are protected. What's more, the supportive reaction of both his parents, who show up and respect Edward's feelings, illustrates the boon in a community of caring others.

Before You Read Together

Edward's tentative toes touching the water tell it all. The inflated water wings also provide a tip-off about how this cub feels about going into the swimming pool. Before reading the book together the first time, let the child notice these cover clues to Edward's feelings. Given the title of *Edward in Deep Water,* also see what your preschooler predicts might happen.

After You Read Aloud

- Ask your child how she feels about swimming lessons, water at the beach or pool, and putting her face under water. Without judging or coaxing, let the preschooler explore her feelings. Together, imagine why some children fear water and how they might show their fear. Explore ways to become less afraid.
- Many children back away from a challenge, simply because they're not ready to meet it. Help the child recall a time when he was in doubt but succeeded. Talk about what made eventual mastery possible.
- Be sure to talk about the fact that water wings don't protect people from drowning.

In the Swim

Like Edward, some children may be vulnerable to mishaps because of other children's actions or lack of good judgment. They need to know that one or more grown-ups will honor their feelings, understand their choices, and do their best to protect them from danger. This is especially true when preschool kids are playing near or in the water.

According to Jon Foss, founder and owner of Foss Swim School in Minnesota (the largest private swim school in the United States), drowning is a swift, silent, and often unseen event. Adults often under-estimate how small a child's lungs are and how quickly they can fill up with water. By relying exclusively on flotation devices, grown-ups unwittingly "teach children to drown." It's the leading cause of death in children from birth to age 4.

Diane Pattridge, a Red Cross–certified water safety instructor who has worked with preschoolers for 25 years, offers important tips worth reviewing and activating prior to any fun excursion to the pool or beach:

- Remain within an arm's length of a preschooler near water, even one wearing flotation devices. Three- and 4-year-olds often over-estimate their abilities, and no matter how good a swimmer, the overly confident child easily can get into trouble.
- Maintain a positive attitude. Fun (with caution) is the focus. With most children under 4, concentrate on water adjustment—floating and moving with confidence—and safety.

* Always use the same cue—1, 2, 3, jump!—as permission to enter the water. Once a child learns to get his face wet, he is likely to love jumping into the water to a waiting grown-up. Ask every adult who interacts with the preschooler in water to use this same cue.

* Teach the basics: a 3- or 4-year-old can master breath control in water for up to 10 seconds and learn how to float on both tummy and back. The motor coordination for swimming freestyle and other strokes comes later.

* Are you nervous or scared around water? A child will pick up on a grown-up's fear of water, so behave confidently and/or seek out professional instruction for you and your child. (In fact, pre-schoolers typically respond to instruction better from a teacher than a parent.)

* Insist that any preschooler wear a certified flotation device (a life jacket, not water wings or float belts) when on a dock or in a boat. Falling into deep water can traumatize a child, making a rescue difficult and perhaps leading to long-term fears.

* Resist comparing one child to others. Respect different readiness levels. Let a child set the pace as you offer him gentle encouragement. Be patient, allowing her control of her environment.

* Repeat the following safety tips with preschoolers—it's never too early to enforce standard rules: Never swim alone. Always swim with an adult. Avoid pushing and running at poolside or dockside. Never jump or dive into a pool without permission. Yell for help instead of jumping in to rescue a drowning child or adult.

Life's a Beach

When was the last time you surprised a preschooler with something totally unexpected? Bring a plastic inflatable pool out of hiding on the dreariest or coldest day of the year. Plop it on a floor inside—perhaps smack dab in the middle of the living room or classroom. Instead of filling the empty pool with water, fill it with pillows for lounging.

Before you take the plunge, look the part and suit up! At the very least, put on sandals, sunglasses, and sun hats. Grab some beach towels, and stir up some lemonade.

Pull out some fun summertime music and, of course, stack some books "poolside." Books about ducks. Books about sharks. Books about boats. Books you know would keep this preschooler happy on a desert island. Dive into them together. Whether you do this or something else equally quirky, the point is to do it now. Here's the chance to send an important message: life's a beach, if you have the will to make it so!

Water Play

The under-5 population finds water play beyond the bathroom as delightful as time in the tub. Everyday items can make a big splash in the kitchen sink or in a dishpan. Beckon young explorers to compare volume in one measuring cup with another, to discover what sinks and what floats, to have a whirl at cleaning plastic toys and dishes, to blend food coloring, and to bathe a doll.

Feeling ambitious? A homemade water play table (24½ inches high) is actually a lot easier to make than you'd think.

You'll need two plastic dishpans, a hammer, several nails, and plywood. (A lumber yard or building supply store clerk can cut the wood to your specifications.) Determine the size of two openings in the plywood tabletop by making them slightly smaller than the surrounding rims (or handles) of the dishpans so that the pans don't slip through the openings, but instead rest securely on the surface. Sand the wood, particularly the edges. Paint the table if you wish.

Fill a "nautical" bag with the following: food coloring to make blue oceans and to create new colors, a funnel, measuring cups and spoons, an empty spray bottle, seashells, a boat to float toy people, and toy cake pans for making mud pies. The table takes up little space in the house in cold weather. Neighborhood kids of all ages will proclaim this magnet for outdoor fun "just ducky!"

Flower Garden

by Eve Bunting, illustrated by Kathryn Hewitt. San Diego: Voyager Books/ Harcourt, 2000.

IN THIS RHYMING TEXT with illustrations as bright as a garden full of blooms, a preschooler enjoys an urban outing to purchase plants. In the company of a loving adult, she carries home their selections. They perch a window box full of the spring flowers on the sill to surprise her mother, who returns home to the blooms and a birthday cake. The story's a perfect example of empowerment. The child is seen as a resource— able to make a contribution.

Before You Read Together

As if the illustrator intended for the reader to be surprised, too, the cover tells little about the story to come. In fact, in the close-up of a preschool-age child admiring flowers, it's impossible to know these plants' location. Ask your preschooler to imagine and name all the places these flowers could possibly be. At story's close, ask if she imagined "a garden in a shopping cart" or "on the checkout stand." Did he predict that flowers could travel on a bus or "sitting on our laps," of all places?

After You Read Aloud

"An inspiration for younger children," according to the *Boston Globe*, this book celebrates surprises and supermarkets, birthdays and bus rides, even shoes with bloomin' linings! See what subject most interests the child. Allow this curiosity to inform your conversation.

How Does YOUR Garden Grow?

For a fun activity together after reading the book, try any of the following suggestions for windowsill gardening. All promise quick results. Helping a preschooler plant and grow a living thing is a fun and inspiring way to create a sense of empowerment.

* Place bean seeds (lentils, limas) on a wet sponge or a folded damp paper towel. Then place the seed and sponge or towel inside a see-through plastic bag or jar and close it. Be sure the sponge or paper towel stays moist. Soon you'll be able to watch the bean break apart and sprout, ready to be transplanted to a pot of soil for continuing growth.

* Insert a few toothpicks halfway into a white or sweet potato. They should be positioned in a circle or line midway around the potato. Suspend the potato by the toothpicks across the opening of a jar of water. The top part of the potato above the toothpicks should be above the rim, while the bottom half sits in water in the jar. Add a bit of plant food if desired. Measure the vine as it grows.

* Cut the tops off a carrot and a beet, making sure a bit of green remains. Lay the vegetables flat in a large saucer of water and watch new leaves appear on both. Talk with your child about the leaves' similarities and differences.

* Cut a sponge or sponges into a desired geometric shape or a figure. Moisten the sponge, and generously sprinkle it with grass seed. Make sure to squirt the sponge with water daily. Within a few days grass will sprout. An alternative is to use an empty soup can, placing soil and grass seed in it, after drawing a face on paper and then affixing it to the can. The grass will grow like hair from the opening, requiring a "haircut" once it grows long enough.

* Fill a glass with just enough water so that when you set an onion on the rim of the glass, the water touches the base of the onion. The onion's pointed end should be facing up. Within a few days, you should see roots extending downward and, shortly after, leaves growing upward.

* For a project with a longer growing time, invite the child to plant nasturtium seeds in a sunny window box, either indoors or out, following package instructions. Over a month's time watch the leaves flourish until flowers bloom—as many as six times the number of seeds. If you pick the blooms, more will follow!

* Here's an idea for growing zucchini in an outdoor patch. Find a plant that has sprouted, grown vines, flowered, and produced a small zucchini. While it's still attached to the vine, slip the small zucchini into a plastic water bottle. The zucchini will conform to the bottle's shape!

Flower Children

Every child deserves up close experiences with flowers, a continuing source of wonder.

* Circle a couple of dates on the calendar. When each arrives, devote part of the day to a visit to someplace alive with things green and growing. Parent and child can set out for a formal public garden, an arboretum, a bird sanctuary, a plant conservatory, or a flower show. A preschool group can enjoy a tour of a working farm, a local nursery, a nursing home courtyard, or the floral business down the block.

* If the grocery store carries flowers, plan on spending five min-utes to sniff them and vote for which ones smell the best. Talk about the names of different flowers on display. Buy a fern if single stems of greenery are for sale. Place it under a sheet of paper, and show your child how to lightly roll or brush a crayon or piece of colored chalk across the paper's surface to reveal the fern's stem and pattern. Using the same color or a new one each time you reposition the fern under the paper, continue the process until the paper is filled with a fernlike design.

* Ask the manager of a floral shop if you and your child can spend ten minutes watching staff members choose flowers and arrange them into bouquets. Ask about the need for refrigeration. Examine different containers that can hold plants or flowers. If possible, buy a single bloom or a small potted plant for the child to tend.
* If you live in northern climes, take a leisurely walk through a greenhouse in winter. The trip can offer a vacation from a gray or all-white world. Purchase an amaryllis bulb, which often comes packaged with pot and soil. Follow directions and store it in a cool dark place, such as a closet, for the required time. Then place it in a sunny spot to watch its dramatic transformation into a towering bright bloom.
* A visit to a farmers' market also provides a supreme sensory experience. Empower the child by giving her or him a dollar or two to purchase something from the assorted wares.

Green Magic

Use a book such as *And the Good Brown Earth* by Kathy Henderson for inspiration. Over the course of a few months—in the right soil and light conditions—you and the child can tend a patch of ground that produces eye-popping miracles from a packet of seeds that costs very little. Consider, for example, some of the offerings at Territorial Seed Company (www.territorialseed.com):

* Early Pink Popcorn (85 days growing time) with beautiful pink kernels that explode into white fluffy morsels when popped or can remain intact as ornamental corn.
* Dill's Atlantic Giant Pumpkin (110 days growing time) that can tip the scales at 800 pounds! Or grow the Prizewinner Pumpkin— at 50 pounds, it's great for carving.
* Miniature Red Bell Peppers (55 days to mature) with up to 75 peppers per plant. They're very sweet and can be eaten whole. Consider planting a rainbow of colors, including Chocolate Beauty, Gourmet Orange, and Purple Beauty, all sweet to taste.

White Flower Farm (www.whiteflowerfarm.com), another source of wonder-working seeds, offered these surprises during one recent planting season:

* Watermelon Moon and Star seeds that in 100 days produce 25-pound dark green melons "covered with yellow moons on a field of tiny yellow stars."
* Kong Sunflower seeds, growing in full sun from 12 to 14 feet high, some visible from a quarter of a mile away. One grower planted a 10-foot-square patch and then cut down the interior stalks, creating a "room" with sunflower walls, a table, and chairs!
* Snack Mix Sunflower seeds, which grow to 6 feet tall in full sun and provide large and tasty sunflower seeds for snack time.

The specific varieties available from suppliers change from season to season, but this gives you a sense of the possibilities. Whatever you plant, have fun reading aloud Mary Ann Hoberman's *Whose Garden Is It?* for the inside scoop on the crowd of critters who claim anyone's garden as their own!

Queenie, One of the Family

. . . .

by Bob Graham. Cambridge, MA: Candlewick Press, 1997.

A YOUNG FAMILY saves the life of a bantam hen. They take her home and name her. "That might have been the end of the story . . . but it wasn't," the author tells us, as he squeezes a series of events between the book's covers: Dad saves a drowning chicken. The hen, Queenie, recuperates in the dog Bruno's basket. Toddler Caitlin takes her first steps. The family finds Queenie's rightful owners. Queenie commutes daily between farm and suburbia, each day laying and leaving an egg for her friends. Mom gives birth to Caitlin's brother. The dog "hatches" a handful of eggs. Queenie reclaims her brood of chicks, and Caitlin adopts one of them! At long last we know why the chicken crossed the road (aided by a freeway overpass)! In this story, the parents empower their toddler by giving her chances to offer assistance and to help with simple chores. They enable Caitlin to feel valued.

Before You Read Together

After reading aloud the title on the cover, puzzle together over the pictured toddler, the enormous dog, and the hen—perched on top of the pooch's head. Have your preschooler guess which one is the Queenie of the title. There are a few giveaways. Notice the smaller version of the chicken, walking across a line just above the title. Point out the set of illustrations of the feathered friend on the back cover, with text that reads: "Nothing can stop Queenie the hen, not a fence . . . or a lake . . . or even a road. Queenie is determined to be one of the family!"

After You Read Aloud

- You'll find that separate illustrations appear on some pages. During the first few readings, use your finger to follow the sequence of actions. Progress from top to bottom and left to right. You'll not only demonstrate the conventional directions to follow when reading books, you'll also help the preschooler to focus on the appropriate part of the story and learn how events follow a sequence.

- Enjoy the antics of both chicken and unconventional family. (It's Dad who knits booties for the coming baby.) Expect to find new details on every visit to this kinder-and-gentler world. From the illustration showing one resolute chicken strutting her stuff to the last, when a toddler takes her first steps in Queenie's direction, prepare for cackles and requests to read the story again!

Enriching "Eggs-periences"

Like sponges, preschoolers absorb details in books, making sense of new information when they go exploring in the world. Activities like the ones that follow provide perfect opportunities to take advantage of the interest that Queenie and her precious eggs inspire:

- ✱ Visit a farm to view chickens and perhaps to collect eggs.
- ✱ In a preschool classroom setting, if you have access to an incubator and directions for warming and turning the eggs, hatch chicks from fertilized eggs (available from Carolina Biological Supply). Make sure you know someone in a rural area willing to take the new arrivals.
- ✱ Make natural egg dyes. You'll need:
  - ☐ A range of liquids, such as cranberry juice, grape juice, apple juice, cooled tea, and coffee
  - ☐ Vinegar
  - ☐ Jars or similar containers
  - ☐ Hardboiled eggs
    Fill each jar with one of the liquids. Add to each jar a tablespoon of vinegar per cup of dye. Place one or more boiled eggs in the jar and soak them for one or two days. Remove the pretty, colorful eggs from the jar.
- ✱ Enjoy an "eggs-tra" special fingerplay:
  Five eggs and five eggs (Hold up all ten fingers.)
  That makes ten.
  Sitting on top is old mother hen. (Fold one hand over the other, the lower in a fist.)

Cluck, cluck, cluck! (Clap hands three times.)
What do I see? (Place hands horizontally above eyes.)
Ten fluffy chicks
As yellow as can be! (Hold up ten fingers again.)

✳ Create a bouncing egg. You'll need:
   ☐ One hardboiled egg
   ☐ Vinegar
   ☐ A drinking glass
   Place the boiled egg in the glass. Fill the glass with vinegar until it covers the egg. Let the egg remain in the vinegar for one or two days. Take it out and let it fall from a low height. It should bounce back because the acid in the vinegar makes the eggshell soft.

Random Acts of Kindness

In this tale, a pair of loving parents lead by example. They could easily choose to neglect responsibility, ignore others' needs, or cite their busy lives to justify doing little or nothing for the other characters. At each point, however, they reveal to their child a better way to be in the world. And each step of the way, they see to it that she has a part to play. The well-being of one lucky chicken is in her pudgy hands as well as theirs. By story's end, we trust that Caitlin will be up to the task of helping care for a pet.

Each of us has opportunities to give to those in need, whether to a child far away or a critter on our doorstep. Be mindful of concrete ways to show the youngest what you do for relatives, coworkers, and strangers. When you give to a charity, explain how the gift will help another. When you contribute your time, money, or talents to causes, find ways to involve the preschooler in your efforts. As in Caitlin's family, see if there are ways to provide a sense of empowerment close to home.

A friend told me that when she was 7 and about to move to another town, on an impulse, her well-meaning mother gave away her dollhouse. Someone had handed it down to my friend. The mother passed it on, in turn. Knowing that the incoming family had very little, her mother later admitted that she'd been motivated by the child's lack of toys. She also may have reasoned that her daughter would soon outgrow the dollhouse. My friend couldn't recall if she'd been encouraged to give her approval. She only remembers how much she missed the beloved plaything and how powerless she felt that a grown-up decided when to give away a belonging of hers.

Young children, like my friend, are just beginning to understand the rewards of giving. Invite preschoolers to play a useful role *without* creating resentment. Listen to their ideas. Include them in decisions. Explore their feelings. Honor their impulses. Notice and celebrate when they initiate random acts of kindness, however small. Empower them to become cheerful givers.

The Pet Project

The presence of a pet teaches young children about friendship, responsibility, loyalty, and empathy. A child who learns to care for an animal gets related practice in understanding how to treat people with gentleness, kindness, and patience. Pets provide a link to nature, teaching respect for other living things. They are a source of comfort and "a sympathetic ear." And an animal's life and death offer lessons about birth, illness, endings, and grief.

Until our kids were older and a cockapoo, Tucker, joined our family, we owned an invisible golden retriever named Gus. This imaginary dog had a water dish in the kitchen and one of those leashes that suspends in the air of its own accord, as if the unseen dog is leading the human behind it. At one point, however, this was not pet enough as far as our children were concerned.

Most preschoolers find the prospect of living with a chicken like Queenie absolutely enchanting. Most adult readers might beg to differ, especially after spying in the illustrations the newspapers spread everywhere to catch random chicken droppings. Alternatives are possible. For preschoolers, experts typically recommend a pet that requires minimal upkeep. (You will be encouraging but not relying on a preschooler to care for the animal. They simply are not developmentally ready to shoulder alone most aspects of daily pet care.) Goldfish and hamsters are reasonable choices to start with in a household or in a classroom.

As we did, you could graduate from pets like goldfish and guinea pigs to a dog or a cat. Make a project of finding out about various breeds before committing to the care of a larger, more complex animal. Whether preschoolers get their own pet or periodically interact with friends' and neighbors' animals, these pointers from experts deserve a nod:

* Provide adult supervision in any room where there's a young child and an animal. Toddlers and preschoolers often have difficulty distinguishing an animal from a toy. They should be taught to be gentle with animals so that the animals are not injured by accident.

* Prohibit roughhousing. Explain that even trained and domesticated animals can be aggressive and try to dominate. Fragile puppies and kittens can resort to play-related biting and scratching.

* Repeatedly inform the child not to disturb an animal when it's sleeping, eating, playing with its own toys, or caring for its babies.

* Teach the child never to put her or his face close to an animal.

* Model responsible pet ownership, giving adequate food, water, exercise, and attention.

* Teach the child to leave an injured animal alone and to seek adult help.

* Help young children recognize signs of behavior in a dog to avoid: hysterical barking, a crouched position, a stiff tail, or a curled lip.

* Instruct the child to always get an adult's permission before touching a neighbor's pet.

* Teach the child how to greet a dog. Remind her to stand still while the dog sniffs her, then slowly to extend her hand, palm up at first, to pet the animal.

* Tell the child not to run away or scream if approached by a strange dog.

* Instruct him to avoid yards in which dogs act high-strung or unfriendly. This warning also goes for any dogs confined in a car or behind a fence, perhaps defending territory.

You Can Do It, Sam

by Amy Hest, illustrated by Anita Jeram. Cambridge, MA: Candlewick Press, 2003.

SURE, SAM'S A BEAR, but preschoolers don't typically get hung up on distinctions between humans and other animals. He and his beloved mama act a lot like us. It's easy to relate to them as they patiently wait for their homemade cakes to come out of the oven. The young bear's eagerness to deliver the cakes to unsuspecting friends is distinctly human. So is his hesitation when the moment to follow through arrives: "All by myself?" he asks tentatively—and "I did it!" he exclaims, once the mission is accomplished. With good reason to celebrate, Mrs. Bear and her boy enjoy two reserved cakes and cocoa at home. Here's a depiction of empowerment assets from beginning to end.

Before You Read Together

A bear, dressed in shiny red boots and a matching jacket, clutches a brightly colored bag. He puts one foot in front of the other as he makes his way across a snowy landscape. The title *You Can Do It, Sam* implies encouragement for a bold mission. Activate your child's curiosity by asking, "What do you suppose is in the bag? Where do you think he's heading?"

After You Read Aloud

- Nothing indicates that each friend who receives the tasty surprise will know who left it. Explore with the child feelings about the value of deeds that go unrecognized.
- After a few readings of the story, ask your preschooler to take a turn telling a story about a bear named Sam who takes cakes all by himself to his friends. If the preschooler is hesitant, take turns telling parts. Help with transitions such as "Once upon a time . . ."

and "They waited . . . and waited . . . and then at last . . ." Emphasize that in the retelling anyone can choose her or his own words
to tell the story. (Some children insist that a familiar story be
repeated word for word. Some may want to tell a different story
about a bear named Sam.)

- Point out the dedication page, in this case at story's end (usually
  it's placed at the front of a picture book). Let the child know that
  often a person who creates a story honors someone he or she
  cares about by naming that person in the book. This dedication
  suggests that two real-life events inspired the tale. Share this
  information.

A Tasty Surprise

Most preschoolers are happy to mimic the plot of the story by making a favorite treat to surprise friends or neighbors. If, however, you and
your young one relish the idea of delivering bundles just like the ones
the bears delivered, here's a recipe for a cake that resembles the illustrated ones.

Find red paper party bags, blue tissue paper, and tags at a stationery
shop or a party store. Snow is optional! Don't forget to have cocoa on
hand and reserve two cakes for the celebration that follows delivery
of the treats. Wrap cakes first in plastic wrap and then in blue tissue,
inserting one per bag. Print "A TASTY SURPRISE" on each tag. Punch
a hole in each bag and each tag. String ribbon through each pair and
tie it. Deliver your treats to some special friends.

CHERRY NUT CAKE

2 cups sugar
2 sticks butter, softened
1 teaspoon vanilla
1 teaspoon almond extract
3 eggs
1 teaspoon baking soda
1 pint sour cream
3 cups flour

1 teaspoon baking powder
1/2 teaspoon salt
1 cup (two 10-ounce jars)
   maraschino cherries, drained
1 cup chopped walnuts or pecans

(continued on next page)

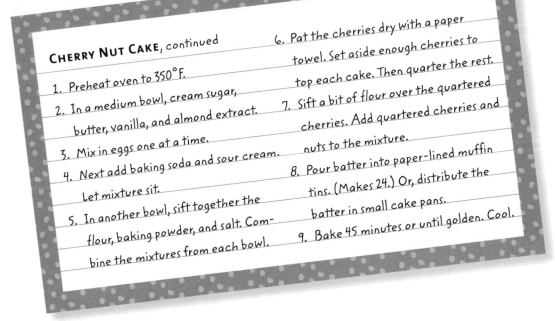

CHERRY NUT CAKE, continued

1. Preheat oven to 350°F.

2. In a medium bowl, cream sugar, butter, vanilla, and almond extract.

3. Mix in eggs one at a time.

4. Next add baking soda and sour cream. Let mixture sit.

5. In another bowl, sift together the flour, baking powder, and salt. Combine the mixtures from each bowl.

6. Pat the cherries dry with a paper towel. Set aside enough cherries to top each cake. Then quarter the rest.

7. Sift a bit of flour over the quartered cherries. Add quartered cherries and nuts to the mixture.

8. Pour batter into paper-lined muffin tins. (Makes 24.) Or, distribute the batter in small cake pans.

9. Bake 45 minutes or until golden. Cool.

Kids Counting

Use Sam's story as a springboard to help a child with counting.

* First help the child count up to 12. If the preschooler's already proficient at this skill, add a twist. Try counting backward from 12 to 1 or try counting to 20 or higher.

* One of the illustrations provides a chance to count cakes on a table (one's hidden in the tissue, one in a bag). Use some colored paper to cut out circles that represent the 12 cakes, putting aside 2 to represent those saved by Sam and his mother for their story-time. Then let the child count to determine how many cakes are still available for friends. Using the cutouts, decide how many places Sam can leave cakes if he leaves two bags at each house. Be sure to pose such challenges by using real objects or drawings and by gauging the child's interest in the process before continuing.

* Expose your preschool-age child to lots of books with numbers. A few additional recommendations are:

    Fish Eyes: A Book You Can Count On by Lois Ehlert

    Ten, Night, Eight by Molly Bang

    26 Letters and 99 Cents by Tana Hoban

    When the Moon Smiled by Petr Horáček

* Make a stack of pictures for counting games. First, find stickers related to a specific subject—dinosaurs, cars, dogs—anything with

at least five types represented. Provide tagboard cut into 4-inch or 5-inch squares. Together, place a single sticker or matching stickers on each square, varying the numbers of one type. (For example, one square might have one cocker spaniel on it, another might have two, and another might have four. Do not exceed six images on one square.) Repeat for each type (poodles, Great Danes, terriers). Together, pull pairs of squares and count the combined totals. Sort sets by a distinguishing feature, such as color or size. Arrange one type in numerical order. (See "Resources" on page 224 for a source of hands-on counting aids.)

Great Expectations

It's not as if the nervous bear in the story had to knock on each door and give a speech to the one who opened it. It's not as if his mother wasn't watching and waiting for him in the truck. Nonetheless, the simplest act can be a very big deal to a younger child. An adult who supplies encouragement and expresses trust in a preschooler—forgiving, too, any mistakes—builds a child's self-confidence, challenge by challenge.

Are the expectations of adults in your child's world in line with his maturity level, her present capabilities? For children in this age group to experience success, you need to remember to:

* Keep activities short and sweet. The attention span of preschoolers is shorter than that of older children and adults. They can tolerate grown-up activities such as shopping, visiting, dining, or game playing only so long and then require a change of focus or activity.

* Take your time. Hurrying is hard on preschoolers. Work schedules, child-care arrangements, classes, and social engagements all contribute to a hectic family life. Grown-ups, with their long legs, often even walk too fast for small children. As the poet Eve Merriam, in her poem "A Lazy Thought," observes, "It takes a lot of slow to grow."

* Issue requests or directions, one by one. Most preschoolers can't take in a rapid-fire list of five directives. A preschooler who hears "Finish your cereal, wash your hands, find your shoes, choose what toy you want to take, and then get your coat" is sure to feel confused. Allow a child to respond to one direction before you offer the next.

* Provide sneak previews. Explain ahead of time what is going to happen at the dentist, at the play, at the preschool, on the outing. Smooth the way by telling why we have to do certain things or why certain behavior is expected.

* Make one-on-one times a priority. A conversation between just the two of you about anything in the world reminds a child that "You belong in this family. You count for something." Daily time in the grown-up's schedule preserved for paying close attention is a must.

Piggy Washes Up

• •

by Carol Thompson. Cambridge, MA: Candlewick Press, 1997.

PROUD PIGGY GIVES US A VIP TOUR of the bathroom, managing to do everything right except leaving the space in any semblance of order. Just like preschoolers! Our guide demonstrates using the toilet, taking a bath, drying off, brushing teeth and hair, weighing in, and dressing in pajamas and a polka-dot bathrobe before bed. This lovable and laughable character makes the tools and practices associated with daily hygiene downright delightful. His example reinforces the importance of adequate self-care as an aspect of empowerment.

Before You Read Together

Look who's in the tub! A funny pig peers over the edge, as interested in the viewer as the viewer is in the cover illustration. Title and picture give tip-offs about the setting to come—someone's bathroom. But whose? Can you and your preschooler figure it out? On the title page, this particular pig, whose clothes are now on the floor, appears to be quite at home in this bathroom. Predict with the child what ways Piggy will wash up, and any other rituals that might come into play.

After You Read Aloud

- Of the activities Piggy demonstrates, which can your child do well? What skill would he like to practice? If you're the parent, make a plan with your child to practice the skill, whether it be toothbrushing, buttoning, or washing behind ears. If you're another caregiver, praise that skill and tell the parent about the child's efforts or interest.

- What are your child's favorite tub toys? Does he own a special toothbrush or comb? Ask your child to see if Piggy uses something similar.
- Can the child explain why we bathe, brush our teeth, use toilet paper, or weigh ourselves? Let her know the purpose of each act if it's not clear.
- Let your finger move from word to word during one reading. The pointing underscores reading conventions (reading left to right), reveals short and long words with corresponding short and long sounds, and establishes which words relate to a particular illustration on a page.

Soap Wins, Hands Down

Your child may go through the motions of hand washing and skip the soap, spending only moments splashing fingers with water. Attempts may be halfhearted and ineffectual, in part, because there is no concept of why the frequent ritual is necessary.

Talk about germs so tiny that they cannot be seen. Explain that they can cause illnesses if they remain on hands, especially if we don't wash after toileting or before eating. Then they can travel from our hands to the food we handle and be put inside our bodies.

Suggest that you conduct an experiment. This activity is adapted from *The Giant Encyclopedia of Preschool Activities for Three-Year-Olds* (see "Acknowledgments" on page 225). Discover if cleaning hands without soap will wash away germs. Ask the little scientist to pretend that the ingredients you put on his hands are germs. You'll need:

☐ Vegetable oil
☐ Cinnamon
☐ Soap and water (cold and warm)
☐ Towels

Place a few drops of oil on the child's hand. Then sprinkle the cinnamon on top of the oil. Encourage him to rub his hands together. Now ask him to quickly wash his hands, using no soap and only cold water. The cinnamon and oil will remain on his hands. Next, add soap and warm water, letting him wash his hands really well. The cinnamon and oil should disappear. Let this discovery serve as a reminder that it takes soap and warm water plus time and effort to get rid of germs.

Dramatic Play

I can recall myself, at 4 or 5, dressed in a doctor's lab coat, actually an old white shirt of my father's. My mother is decorating the pocket with a bright Red Cross symbol. This simple costume somehow authenticates my play. It gives everything I do next—listening to a doll's heartbeat, prescribing medicine, or giving a shot—an authority I didn't feel before. Like the characters in books that model good health habits—in costume, in character, the child plays out positive values.

In our son's preschool years, nothing got more use than the hinged costume box in the bedroom window seat. If a 3-year-old trying on a tutu or fingering a feather boa comes to mind, you're partially right. Through all his transformations as superheroes, working stiffs, mythical beings, and role models, such as doctors and dads, he donned his share of girlie glitz as well.

Both boys and girls can enjoy sporting hard hats one day and sparkly jewels the next. I find it unsettling when we limit dramatic play to "dress-up." Dress-up, in turn, means froufrou or fancy, and fancy often means girls only. Make-believe or pretend play with a wide range of costumes and props is a wonderful way to act out situations, familiar and unfamiliar. A time-honored example involves predicting and re-playing visits to the doctor's office.

Yes, through make-believe or dramatic play, the child can slay dragons or go to the ball. As important, however, are the chances to be prepared for or to resolve feelings about real-life experiences, such as getting sick or getting shots. Even the youngest child's simple house-keeping play involves taking the part of the parent who keeps the (doll) babies healthy and happy and free from harm.

Join in and model techniques or exchanges that extend the play. If a child seems ready, create a pretend waiting room where stuffed animals wait their turn, or provide a small tablet and pencil for writing out prescriptions. Ask a few questions (e.g., "How could the doctor make him feel better?") and suggest ways to expand the play.

Older preschoolers like to try on roles of others in the community. They appreciate a greater range of props, pretend scenarios, and open-ended questions to enrich a form of play that builds motor, verbal, social, and cognitive skills. Invite the child to mimic the actions of characters in favorite stories. Give her a rubber pig snout or a toy pig, for instance, to enliven tired bedtime rituals as the little Piggy "washes up"!

Props, Please

To encourage play that allows children to try on positive roles for size, furnish a laundry basket or large suitcase with props. Collect yard sale or thrift store finds. Make simple garb.

Other than a toy stethoscope, for example, "medical props" include easy-to-find items—cotton swabs, a scale, a flashlight, a homemade eye chart, bandages, gauze, popsicle sticks, a pad, a pencil, and dolls. Other stories will inspire preschoolers to put themselves in the shoes of a range of characters. Anticipate this interest in pretend play and role-playing by providing a treasure trove of props:

* **Capes:** Kids crave black ones as magicians, red ones as super-heroes or Red Riding Hood, and purple ones with a collar of white fake fur as royalty. Don't know a soul who sews? Try this:

    1. With about 1½ yards of the desired color(s), measure the distance between the child's neckline and knees (or ankles) and add 6 inches to the desired length. Determine the width by tripling the inches from shoulder to shoulder.

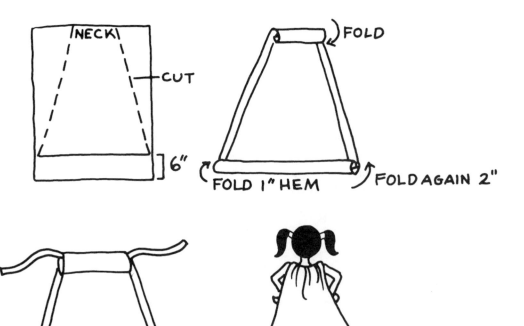

2. Next measure the inches around the child's neck, adding 6 inches to that length.

3. Mark the end points of that line, centered at the top edge, for the collar.

4. Draw a diagonal line from the end point at the left top to the left bottom corner of fabric. Repeat with a diagonal line from the right top end point to the right bottom corner.

5. Cut along these diagonals.

6. Fold over all four sides with 1-inch hems, using iron-on hem adhesive.

7. Repeat by folding 2-inch-wide hems on all sides but the top (collar). Secure the hems with the hem adhesive,

8. Fold a 2-inch top hem over an 18-inch length of ribbon (for a tie) and hand sew a line beneath it so that the ribbon, when tied, gathers the neckline fabric.

* **Felt fabric costumes:**
  1. Buy enough felt to cover the child's body from shoulder to shoulder and neck to ankle. Be sure to double the length so you have enough fabric for front and back.
  2. Fold the fabric in half and cut an opening for the head.
  3. Cut fringe or add details with a marker.
  4. Cinch with a belt, and you get an instant elf (green felt), knight (gray felt), or ladybug (red felt with black dots glued on).

* **Hats:** Popular headgear includes a crown, a hard hat, a ball cap, a straw hat, a wig, a top hat, a chef's hat, a safari hat, an engineer cap, and the like.

* **Found objects:** Old standbys include glasses without lenses, jewelry, masks, wands (for a magician's wand, paint a dowel black with a white tip; for a fairy wand, attach a foil star), badges, vests, adult shirts with sleeves cut or folded over, scarves, uniform hats, and canteens.

* **Interactive toys:** Puppets, dolls, model figures, or stuffed animals give imagination wings.

Empowerment Bonus Best Bets

- **All by Myself!** by Aliki. New York: HarperCollins, 2000.

- **Can I Help?** by Marilyn Janovitz. New York: North-South Books, 1996.

- **Good Dog, Paw!** by Chinlun Lee. Cambridge, MA: Candlewick Press, 2004.

- **I Can't Talk Yet but When I Do . . .** by Julie Markes, illustrated by Laura Rader. New York: HarperCollins, 2003.

- **Mole and the Baby Bird** by Marjorie Newman, illustrated by Patrick Benson. New York: Bloomsbury Children's Books, 2002.

- **My Mama Sings** by Jeanne Whitehouse Peterson, illustrated by Sandra Speidel. New York: HarperCollins, 1994.

- **Wilfrid Gordon McDonald Partridge** by Mem Fox. Brooklyn, NY: Kane/Miller, 1996.

Boundaries & Expectations

Preschoolers benefit from a clear understanding of boundaries in family life as well as in the neighborhood and other out-of-home situations. At the same time, while the significant others in their lives set limits for young children's greater good, they encourage age-appropriate habits, tasks, and interactions. They give little ones a sense of mastery. The most effective way to uphold these great expectations is to act as role models ourselves.

• •

POSITIVE ASSOCIATIONS WITH READING and books come from adults who model their enthusiasm and commitment. Your expectations influence a child's attitudes about book use. The norm should be reading to preschoolers for pleasure 15 to 30 minutes per day.

We need to examine our assumptions about what kinds of books are suitable for young children. Parents and teachers must make sure not to limit access to rich vocabulary and engaging stories. If one limits preschool fare to board books or bargain table finds, preschoolers are apt to quickly lose interest.

Be patient with a child learning to listen and to pay attention, without a competing TV or other distractions. Experiment to see if the child needs more sophisticated stories to remain engaged. Do not assume, however, that books with few illustrations and lots of text will speed a young child's progress.

The recommended asset-rich titles honor varying maturity levels of preschoolers. While organized with 3-year-old and 4-year-old sensibilities in mind, there are examples suitable for younger children and many appealing stories that 5- and 6-year-olds can enjoy, too.

How Do Dinosaurs Say Good Night?

• •

by Jane Yolen, illustrated by Mark Teague. New York: The Blue Sky Press/ Scholastic, 2000. (Spanish edition: *¿Cómo dan las buenas noches los dinosaurios?*)

WITH ENGAGING RHYME and over-the-top illustrations of ever-popular dinosaurs, author Jane Yolen and illustrator Mark Teague humorously depict bedtime behavior that no "self-respecting" prehistoric creature would ever "resort to in order to stay up." ("Does he mope, / does he moan, / does he sulk, / does he sigh? / Does he fall on the top of his covers and cry?") They then reveal the peaceful nighttime rituals of every "domesticated" dimetrodon, stegosaurus, and T. rex.

Grown-ups and children may laugh at the dinosaurs who raise a ruckus at bedtime, but the message, by story's end, is clear: boundaries and expectations are part of this recurring event. It's about loving with limits set for the good of the young—reptilian or otherwise.

Before You Read Together

Despite the illustrator's imposing tyrannosaurus, perched on a bed about one-fourth its size, the cover signals that great fun lies ahead. Together, count up the cues that promise a whimsical romp through the pages: the nervous look on Rex, not on the human mom in the doorway, who, with hand on hip, is clearly in charge; the bear and beloved blanket clutched for comfort in the dinosaur's claws; the family pooch, cool as a cucumber; the childlike drawing of a dinosaur, a rocker, and toys depicting a child's room, albeit a monstrous one's. To extend the promise of nonstop silliness, the endpapers inside the covers feature labeled dinosaurs blowing bubbles, jumping on the bed, and even reading!

After You Read Aloud

- Return to the illustrations and together find letters that spell out the name of each featured dinosaur. You'll see them on items such as a wall pennant, a line of alphabet blocks, and a bed's headboard.
- After you've enjoyed the story a number of times, invite your child to say the rhyming word at the end of a verse.
- For fun, act out the meaning of verbs such as *mope, moan,* and *sulk,* or demonstrate for the child how readers can find the exact meaning of a word by looking it up in a dictionary.
- Talk about favorite dinosaurs or favorite illustrations. Together note the reactions of the illustrated pets.

Sleepy-time Rituals

Any number of rituals helps to ease the transition from active play in the company of others to turn-out-the-lights time. Putting in place a predictable set of preliminary steps sets the stage for sleep.

At preschool or in the child-care setting, regularly singing a familiar song as children move to their cots or rugs or turning on a simple sound machine that mimics ocean surf or rain signals a time to rest.

Read-aloud time with familiar fare, shown to slow the heartbeat and calm the listener, is a time-honored bedtime ritual. Include classics that soothe, rather than excite. The following ones, with their rhythmic and repetitive format, fill the bill:

Goodnight Moon by Margaret Wise Brown
Hush! by Minfong Ho
Hushabye by John Burningham
Time for Bed by Mem Fox

Tuck-in time is sacred time that is set aside for loving attention from one or more primary caregivers in a child's life. Here's the golden opportunity to briefly recall a highlight of the day, to remind your child of something you value about her, and, before he sleeps, to reach out with a reassuring backscratch, a hug, or kiss. Make sure that videos or CDs, however relaxing, don't take the place of *your presence* at the end of each day.

Dino-Might!

Do you know somebody smitten with dinosaurs? I found it amazing that my own son, who was busy perfecting two-syllable words only a year earlier, could rattle off names like ankylosaurus at age 3. Suddenly he was capable of coolly explaining the differences between carnivores and herbivores to his sister's 3rd-grade teacher and class. When he found that a cake decorator had put the wrong number of claws on a tyrannosaurus atop his birthday cake, he was decidedly miffed. For dinosaur fans, this book (and others) can be a springboard to spending time in dinosaur country.

* Turn inexpensive plastic dinosaurs into props that stimulate use and growth of language. Encourage the preschooler to identify each (with your help, if necessary) as you print every name on a separate label or index card. Then help her create a museum. Display specimens and labels on various pedestals (blocks) or in a diorama (a shoebox turned on its side works well). Make a landscape backdrop for the box using crayons or construction paper.

* Use these models to explore concepts of size, type, and number. Invite him to arrange the creatures in order of size, in a set that possesses a similar characteristic (e.g., meat eaters), or in groups to see how many of any one dinosaur he owns (e.g., one triceratops, one pterodactyl, two tyrannosauruses, four dimetrodons).

* Let her dictate a simple story involving a dinosaur. Preschoolers' tales can be gross or gory, so don't be surprised if the main character gets eaten or the predator gets its due. (In fact, at this developmental stage, children need to know that "evil" will be punished. Their outrageous endings or scary stories are normal.)

* If you have the opportunity, visit a museum that displays a dinosaur skeleton so that the preschooler gets a better sense of the size and might of these extinct beasts. Or research the height of a dinosaur of choice and reveal its size by premeasuring and drawing an outline with food coloring on snow or using thick bright yarn on grass. Compare it to the preschooler's height or dimensions.

Dinosaur Dig

A visit to the butcher for an interesting assortment of bones, including some big ones, can launch a project sure to thrill budding paleontologists. Younger preschoolers will be happy to dig for these "dinosaur bones," thoroughly cleaned and loosely buried by an adult in a sandbox or some play dirt. Send one or more adventurers "into the field"—a backyard or preschool play area—armed with a canteen, a backpack of provisions (a snack), note pads and pencils for scribbling info or tracing the outlines of bones they unearth, and utensils (wooden or plastic spoons, strainers) for sifting and digging. Count the bones they've discovered once they return to "camp."

Older preschoolers will appreciate a more ambitious "dig" that can take place over time, just as work in a museum lab does. Line a medium-size box with a plastic bag or similar liner. Mix up a batch of plaster of Paris according to package instructions. Add mulch or dirt to the mixture. Cover the bottom of the lined box with half of the mixture. Position the bones and pour the remaining mixture over them. Let everything dry before removing the box and liner.

Supervise the use of small screwdrivers and other "tools" to chip away at the block. Provide small safety goggles for such work. (See "Resources" on page 224 for information on where to find such goggles.) Swim goggles also can sometimes fill the bill. Dry paintbrushes can brush away dust and reveal emerging bone. Magnifying glasses aid in the detail work.

Now I'm Big

by Margaret Miller. New York: Greenwillow Books, 1996.

AUTHOR AND PHOTOGRAPHER MARGARET MILLER has produced an appealing book filled with simple specific examples of how far a group of young children has come since infancy. Young narrators contrast typical pastimes as babies with their present-day activities and accomplishments. The reader returns repeatedly to a group portrait of six children, in which a different child's face is highlighted each time to identify the source of the words and pictures that describe this individual child's progress. All but a few experiences (e.g., "I ride a brown pony") are universal. With obvious pride, they undertake challenging tasks and do well, meeting positive expectations. This book is a reminder to children who may feel very small at times that, like the proud narrators, they, too, are changing and growing.

Before You Read Together

The title and a montage of color photographs on the cover (repeated on the back) reveal the thrust of this book. The preschooler with whom you are sharing it will likely feel like a member of the "big kids' club" when seeing the various young children drinking juice from a glass, confidently jumping from play equipment, and getting dressed without help. In fact, he or she may decide to predict what examples the featured children will focus on when you read the book for the first time.

After You Read Aloud

- On a piece of paper, list with the child a few examples of how she spent her days as a baby, beginning with the words "When I was a baby . . ." just as the book does. Then print the words "Now I'm big! I . . ." and have her respond about what she's proud or happy she can do now. Let her see what her own words look like in neat printing. You may wish to affix (with re-movable poster tape) her contribution to the front or back end-papers of the book to review during future readings.

A Big Deal

No one ever really outgrows the occasional need for someone to make a big deal of her or his presence on the planet. One way to do this is to create a special album that celebrates the growth of the child dear to your heart. The child-care provider or preschool teacher can do some-thing similar, but instead feature all of the children in a group, just as the author of *Now I'm Big* has done. Bring together:

- ☐ A three-ring binder, preferably with a see-through customizable front cover (sold in stores as "view" binders)
- ☐ Several three-ring, transparent sheet protectors
- ☐ Notebook paper or decorative paper with three holes added using a hole puncher
- ☐ 8½-x-11-inch montage of photos of the child in action, mixed in with a couple of baby photos. Photocopy the photos onto paper if you wish to save the originals.
- ☐ List of favorites—toys, foods, colors, pastimes, places to visit—as told to a grown-up
- ☐ Sheet(s) of paper on which the phrases "When I was a baby, I . . ." and "NOW I'M BIG. I . . ." appear repeatedly on separate lines. Photocopy several times and cut out the phrases in strips.
- ☐ An assortment of current and past photos (duplicated or photo-copied) of the child (and much-loved objects)
- ☐ Glue stick

To begin, slip the montage of photos into the notebook's front cover to mimic the cover of *Now I'm Big*. Or, if your child prefers, feature a homemade self-portrait on the cover. In either case, add NOW I'M BIG as a title. Let the child glue the paper strips printed with phrases onto blank pages and place in the binder. Neatly copy down his exact words as he completes some of these phrases now and some later in the year. Date each entry. Empower her to decide on the items, artwork, or pho-tos to add to her statements. Add the favorites list, with the preschooler dictating the content. Tuck mementos, artwork, and pictures into the sheet protectors until you and the little scrapbooker revisit this ongoing project.

Tees for Two

When a new baby has arrived in a household, preschoolers often must adapt to changed circumstances and compete for time with weary pre-occupied parents. Is it any wonder so many can regress temporarily to babylike behaviors. They need special attention and reassuring signs that they still matter, too. You can meet the challenge in numerous ways.

* Before the birth, initiate a T-shirt project. Together, decorate one for the coming baby and one for the sibling-to-be, using white shirts of appropriate sizes. Insert a piece of cardboard between the front and back of each shirt. Pour different colors of fabric paint onto separate paper plates. Using sponge cutouts or the child's outstretched palm, make a design on the back or front of the child's T-shirt.

  Let the shirt dry for at least a day. Print I'M THE BIG BROTHER (or SISTER) or Now I'M BIG on the child's shirt front. Use a fabric pen or sponge-paint the words over a stencil. Your child may want you to add a few words that describe personal traits or talents: . . . and I'M KIND, FUNNY, HELPFUL. Dry completely. Sponge-paint designs on the baby's T-shirt, waiting until you know the baby's gender to add I'M THE LITTLE BROTHER (or SISTER) on the front. Wash both T-shirts before they are worn.

  Our oldest child liked to wear such a shirt whenever visitors came to see the new arrival. It was a visual reminder that she counted, too. Let your child wear the T-shirt when she needs to feel important.

* Put her feelings into words through books, such as Kevin Henkes's *Julius, the Baby of the World; Big Brother, Little Brother* by Penny Dale; or *Oonga Boonga* by Frieda Wishinsky, which suggest to important older siblings that the situation will eventually improve.

* If you're a parent, ask a compassionate friend, relative, or youth to provide an outing or two for your older child, without it appearing that you only want to be with the newborn.

* If the preschooler persists in babylike behavior, cheerfully suggest that he role-play for a morning, providing a concrete reminder—as he stays in bed for needed naps, eats a narrow range of mushy foods, plays with few toys—that big is better.

* Provide relief from confinement or competition and enroll her in a fun weekly activity.
* Find time to be together and encourage him to express feelings that come and go. Repeat to yourself and/or a beleaguered child, especially on a hard day: "This, too, shall pass."

Affirmations

Authors and researchers Betty Hart and Todd R. Risley made groundbreaking discoveries in their landmark report *Meaningful Differences in the Everyday Experience of Young American Children*. A primary one is the importance, from an early age, of a language-rich environment with daily talking and reading aloud. They also confirmed the powerful effect that instances of positive feedback versus criticism or prohibitions have on a child's chances for success. Families who offered frequent encouragement and praise from an early age, giving attention to strengths, skills, and behavior, later witnessed higher achievement in their kids. Families that normally made disparaging, critical, and prohibitive comments and peppered exchanges with "no's" and "don'ts" unwittingly made it less likely their children would succeed in school. The researchers' findings confirm that parents' controlling or critical comments have negative effects in the long run.

For a week, monitor what you say to young children. I kept a record as a classroom teacher. Each time I said something specific to a child about a personality trait, a helpful gesture, an accomplishment, or a challenge met, I put a check mark by the name of the child I'd just affirmed. If you do likewise, you may be surprised. There could be a marked difference between the totals for one of the children versus another. You may discover that you give little positive feedback. Begin noticing. Begin affirming. Marvel aloud each day about the gifts each child brings to your life.

Don't Let the Pigeon Drive the Bus!

by Mo Willems. New York: Hyperion Books for Children, 2003.

IN THIS CALDECOTT HONOR BOOK, Emmy Award–winning writer and animator Mo Willems (*Sesame Street, Sheep in the Big City*) provides children with the rare opportunity to "be the boss." A persistent pigeon pleads for permission to drive the very bus that the driver asks the young reader to keep intact until he returns. Cleverly, the author has created an interactive work for children that prompts them to set boundaries despite one bird's efforts to test understandable limits. In the process, the kids fulfill adult expectations that they know what's reasonable.

Before You Read Together

The bird on the cover appears as a childlike drawing—stick legs, a "head" composed of a crudely drawn circle and, within it, another circle that is all eye, with a beak added on, and a single line that suggests a wing. If any doubt remains about this bird being a comical one, the illustrator further establishes the tone by containing the silly title within a cartoon balloon. Make sure you talk about the endpapers' wordless illustration, just inside, as the bird imagines itself driving the same bus. The action begins before the title page, with the driver addressing the reader. Point out cartoonish features.

After You Read Aloud

- It's up to the adult reader to pull out all the stops and play the pigeon to the hilt—wheedling, whining, complaining, cajoling, and, thanks to the young child's refusal to cave, crumbling until another vehicle comes into view. The child will delight in the grown-up taking the role of the pesky pigeon (wondering, per-haps, if you had lots of practice whining and wheedling while you were growing up).

- The pigeon's methods can inspire discussion between you and the child about unacceptable behavior, good reasons for setting limits (in this case, to protect bus and pigeon), and praise for the child's firm stand.

Whine Control

Dramatize the pigeon's wearying behavior and playfully give the child a dose of how it feels to be on the receiving end. Invite the child to ask for something, using a whining voice. (Since whining is especially com-mon in 2- and 3-year-olds, it's a request most preschoolers can fulfill!) You might make a face and hold your ears. Reveal that this kind of talk-ing is just not something peace-loving pigeons, big boys, or big girls do. Next, invite him to ask for something in a regular voice. Note the improvement, and praise the difference.

When you are out and about with your child, if you observe another child whining, quietly point out the behavior, making eye contact with your preschooler and shaking your head sadly as the two of you witness this alternate and unproductive form of "pigeon" English.

Setting limits actually helps our kids to feel safe, so firm guidelines are important. Children typically tend to whine when they're feeling frustrated, defeated, overwhelmed, disappointed, or unsuccessful at something. A whine is a plea for focused attention or relief from a too-challenging situation.

During one day, monitor how many times you say "No." No's re-peated in succession can lead to frustration. It's a quick way to set limits, but the word loses its potency when overused. In *kids are worth it!*, Barbara Coloroso suggests alternative phrases. One, for example, is "Give me a minute . . ." This phrase signals that you will, in fact, think about the pros and cons. Another is "Yes, later." It promises a treat, a read-aloud session, or attention at a more appropriate time.

Experts note that whining can make adults feel as if they've failed a child. They may need to take a deep breath. Next, they can give a focused minute or two to be attentive to the tired child's needs, quietly and calmly asking her to speak in a regular voice. Parents and teachers can show that the child has been heard by repeating what he's said and responding reasonably or taking action to lessen the frustration. Obviously, in interactions with our children, we can't always do the equivalent of letting the pigeon drive the bus. But we can take seriously the needs or feelings that prompt the whining and encourage children to use better ways to express wants or needs.

Move On Back!

Recently our son recalled the excitement he felt as a 3-year-old when his dad took him to work on the city bus. We had a good laugh after he confessed it was this very ride that had convinced him that his daddy was the smartest man in the world. After all, his father not only knew just when and where a bus would stop for the two of them, but he correctly guessed how much money the driver wanted him to put in his machine! He knew just where to sit and, miraculously, he managed to board a bus that took them just a block from their destination!

Every child should have a chance to ride a bus. If you live in a rural area, when you take a trip into the city create an excuse to ride from one site to another. If you live in the suburbs, you may be accustomed to driving everywhere—the bus representing a less efficient means to get things done. Let the bus trip itself be the thing you "do."

Sing verses of "The Wheels on the Bus" while you wait for it to come. Have exact change ready, and lift the child up to deposit it. Make a plan to survey all the shoes of passengers on board and decide on your favorite pair. Enjoy the chance to "move on back" to sit in a place where you can study all kinds of people and guess where they are going. Converse with one or two.

Mud Pies

Sometimes we say "No" or set limits, not because an activity is potentially harmful, but because it's inconvenient or just plain messy. When's the last time, for instance, that you urged your preschooler to go play in the mud?

I don't know if Charlotte Pomerantz's wonderful book *The Piggy in the Puddle* or a big square of black dirt awaiting plants at the back door inspired the play, but making mudpies was the main attraction for one of our kids for days when she was 4. This dirt-cheap activity requires only soil and water, supplied by a rain shower, a garden hose, or a half-full pitcher. Setting up an indoor version in the preschool classroom

Curses!

Do you get the feeling that if the pathetic pigeon in this story knew any cuss words, the bird might have used them for added impact? In the real world, preschoolers rather than pigeons have been known to utter one, often out of the blue.

While children over the age of 6 who use foul language are usually well aware of the shock value and, often, the word's meaning, younger ones may be quite innocent of the resulting impact. The unexpected delivery, the very sight of a cherubic child cursing, catches many grown-ups off guard and, despite the shock, the temptation may be to laugh.

Avoid laughing. It signals that the curse has entertainment value for big people, and you can bet it will be repeated. Also resist outrage, followed by punishment. This reaction ignores the developmental stage of preschoolers who innocently experiment with all kinds of words and their effect on older kids and grown-ups.

Experts in child development consistently offer this advice:

1. Model appropriate language to set a standard of behavior. Be honest about your remorse if you do slip up.
2. Send clear messages about how you feel about inappropriate language.
3. Don't make a big deal of the utterance. Remind the child of any age that such language is unacceptable to you. Say, "We don't use words like that," and move on.
4. Monitor TV programming, an influence on the child's vocabulary. Show your disapproval of the inappropriate language that's overheard.

proved popular, too, with girls and boys, especially after a reading of Pomerantz's funny book as well as access to *Mud Pies and Other Recipes* by Marjorie Winslow. One favorite was her recipe for Pine Needle Upside-Down Cake. Kids are perfectly capable of creating their own concoctions as well.

Find a patch of dirt outside or partially fill a dishpan with potting soil. Provide water to pour into the dirt, as needed, to make mud of a pleasing consistency. Assemble any number of "containers"—bottle caps, paper cups and milk cartons cut by an adult to a height of 2 or 3 inches, muffin tins, or toy pans. Add pine needles, small twigs, flower petals, delicate leaves, tiny pebbles, and/or berries to mix into or garnish the creations.

Let the chefs play with the mud and fill the containers, setting them near a heater or in the sun to dry and harden. Gently remove them from containers and serve on large leaves to admiring grown-ups or plush bears. Later, leave the homemade banquet outside for the fairies. Or, see what happens when one adds warm water to the solid mud pies. Then start all over again!

Trashy Town

• •

by Andrea Zimmerman and David Clemesha, illustrated by Dan Yaccarino. New York: HarperCollins, 1999.

MR. GILLY DOES A STELLAR JOB of collecting trash by the school, in the park, and by the fire station. Once he has managed to clean the whole town, there's only one more thing to clean up—himself! He loves his work and serves as one of the role models in a community, embodying what's expected of and valued in young children.

Before You Read Together

The child may identify that a taxi and tall buildings on the cover suggest a city setting. He may notice the big garbage truck under the title *Trashy Town* with trash cans and a couple of scampering rats. If you've preread the story, offer a comment or two to provide a tantalizing preview: "Wait until you see what the trash collector juggles!" or "I like finding the rats on each page!"

After You Read Aloud

- A prereader can take a cue from the red color of the word *STOP!* and shout it out whenever your finger points to it. Most children will also delight in recognizing the word *NO,* since it always appears in yellow at the same place on a page. This early experience of "reading" is both fun and empowering.
- Preschoolers, who soon catch on to the repeated refrain at each stop, enjoy chanting, "Dump it in, smash it down, drive around the Trashy Town!"
- Young children often take words literally. Alternate the word *trash collector* with *trashman* when talking about the book, just

as you use terms such as *firefighter* and *police officer* to send a message to both boys and girls that they can grow up to be anything they want.

Wormville

One of the most important creatures on the planet lives beneath our feet. The lowly worm, often only prized for its usefulness at the end of a fishhook, is the ultimate recycler. Slithering in the soil and compost heaps that are their cities, they make magic. Without wheels or trash bins, they rid us of waste, turning it into fertile ground. For a hilarious take on the worm's lofty calling, read aloud *Diary of a Worm* by Doreen Cronin.

The next time you and your child spy a worm in a rain puddle, bend down to observe it. Study worms under a magnifying glass with one or more preschoolers. Better yet, make a small composter, that "magical" container in which decaying matter transforms into rich fertilizer, and watch worms do their thing. You'll need:

- ☐ A large plastic fish tank, a medium-size terrarium, or a jumbo plastic soda bottle, preferably clear/translucent so that the child can observe worms at work
- ☐ Potting soil, damp shredded newspaper (1-inch strips), sand, healthy leaves, and/or mulch
- ☐ Vegetable peelings, eggshells, coffee grounds, other organic matter (no meat, dairy, or citrus products)
- ☐ A piece of black fabric or a black plastic bag to fit over the whole container
- ☐ Worms found in the garden, the bait shop, or a vericomposting store (learn about an alternate use of red worms and bin composters at www.wormpoop.com)

1. After telling the child about how worms recycle leftovers and other organic/natural materials, making soil "good as new," assemble the needed items for a composter. You may wish to add a brick or other solid object in the center so that the resident worms are more likely to be viewable, moving about a *clear* container's sides in the dark.
2. Fill the chosen container halfway with loose potting soil and improve it by mixing in leaves, shredded paper, mulch, and/or sand.

3. Add worms. Wrap the clear container and cover any opening with the black fabric or bag to simulate the dark underground home that worms require. Keep in a cool place.

4. Continue, at weekly intervals, to supply the wriggly recyclers with kitchen food scraps and organic matter, keeping the contents moist, but not wet.

5. Marvel as the worms transform the "garbage" into soil.

Litter Patrol

Mr. Gilly in this story (and the talking garbage truck in *I Stink!* by Kate McMullan) may inspire the child to become a member of the litter patrol. If desired, supply a cap to wear as Mr. Gilly does when on the job.

Perhaps the little one is able, with gentle reminders, to take on the responsibility of emptying small wastebaskets once or twice a week. With your supervision, she may be happy to organize bottles and cans in the recycling bin. He can keep an eye out for litter in the yard or inside, even making a sign, with your help, that offers people a friendly reminder: PLEASE DON'T LITTER. Invite a group of children to join you and the preschooler on a special day to pick up neighborhood litter, capping the cleanup mission with a story and refreshments.

Challenge children to put on their plates only what they can eat, with second helpings always an option. Invite them to keep tabs on how much of their food goes from plate to garbage, even weighing the total on a food scale, if you wish, and striving to reduce uneaten portions.

Let the child be on the lookout for litter wherever you go, disposing of anything that isn't sharp and that doesn't carry lots of germs such as used tissues or half-eaten foods out of containers. If you two haven't thanked your trash collector, express your gratitude for a weekly job well done.

Helping Hands

Most young children want to feel valued as participating members of the family or community. Sometimes the limited ways they can serve are a source of frustration or comparison for preschoolers who aspire to help in bigger ways—especially if older siblings play a greater role. The solution is not to give children chores or challenges for which they are not developmentally ready, leading to greater frustration or failure. Rather, highlight the value of what they are able to do.

Show a child in a concrete way that little things add up, that every effort counts. The helping-hand wreath is an art project that motivates and engages kids. A parent can make one at home to represent the efforts of a single child, or teachers and care providers can use one to celebrate the collective contributions of members of a group. Assemble:

☐ Two bowls of different sizes, around 6 and 9 inches in diameter (or a compass to make circles of two sizes)

☐ Piece of foam board, available at craft stores and art supply shops

☐ Fabric in different patterns, saturated or sprayed with fabric stiffener and allowed to dry or scrapbooking paper or gift wrap in a variety of designs (glued to poster board)

☐ Glue, poster tape, or straight pins

☐ Marker or pencil for outlining the child's hand

☐ Scissors

☐ String

1. On the foam board, draw an outline of the larger bowl. Cut out the circle.

2. Draw an inner circle, using another smaller bowl (or a compass) that produces a foam band or wreath at least 3 inches wide. Cut out the inner circle.

3. Trace the outline of the child's hand(s) many times on the fabric or paper.

4. Cut out the handprints. You might invite an older child to do the honors.

5. Mount the bare foam wreath with string. Each time the child extends a helping hand, let her choose a handprint to attach to the wreath. Overlap hands as you add them.

Officer Buckle and Gloria

• •

by Peggy Rathmann. New York: G. P. Putnam's Sons, 1995.

IN THIS CALDECOTT HONOR BOOK, the dog that costars with Officer Buckle is a rare breed. Gloria, the police dog, adds pizzazz to the officer's presentations about safety tips on visits to schools and child-care centers. Unbeknownst to her master, she dramatizes his tips behind him as he speaks, rocketing into the air, for example, when he warns children, "NEVER leave a THUMBTACK where you might SIT on it!" When he discovers that the pair's popularity with kids is due to her shenanigans, he's upset. But after the reminder that his message is important, he's willing to share the glory. Here's another role model who sets the bar high when it comes to expectations.

Before You Read Together

A bespectacled police officer looks befuddled as kids, around the stage where he stands, gaze upward. They're tracking the amazing flip of one talented dog. Perhaps your child will guess that this is Gloria. Stars border three sides of the front cover, each bearing a picture and tiny printing. The fourth side displays the name of the person who made the story and pictures. Ask questions to determine if your child understands that a real person thinks up the story and that this author or another artist puts the artwork on paper. Explain that a printer makes many more copies for others to enjoy.

After You Read Aloud

- The front and back endpapers inside the covers provide a perfect chance to talk about reasons for certain safety rules. Encourage the child to randomly pick a couple of tips to talk about during each encounter. Invite the child to contribute safety tips of her own or from the book to put on mounted stars.

- School-age children send letters to Officer Buckle. Let the child know that someday he will know how to print words, too. In the meantime, ask if he would like you to print a letter to someone, using his own thoughts and words. Suggest that he draw a picture to go with it.

Pretzels

Officer Buckle treasures the flood of children's letters, telling him why they value him. A weekly ritual known as "Pretzels," originated by educator Ruth Charney, is a proven and powerful practice for providing affirmations for participants from kindergarten through middle school. If the children are 4 or older, you might consider adapting and adopting this weekly ritual.

In this activity, preschoolers focus only on positive comments to and from kids and grown-ups as part of a family meeting or during a preschool session. (School-age kids also can request a pretzel from someone whose actions have made them feel sad or upset; for a description of this second stage for older kids, see the 2002 edition of *Teaching Children to Care* by Ruth Charney.) For each child, you'll need a bag of pretzel sticks and a paper cup.

1. Let the child count out 10 small pretzel sticks per cup. Give one set to each participant.
2. Encourage children to resist eating any pretzels until the circle ritual is complete.
3. Form a circle sitting in chairs or on the floor. Adults may participate, not only helping to model statements but also hearing from children whom they have helped in some way.
4. Going around the circle, ask each participant if he or she would like to give one pretzel as a thank-you to someone for something the person did that made the child feel good. Focus on behavior during that day. (Aidan let me try on his cape. Tonya hugged me when I fell down. José shared his crackers. Karim acted silly and made me laugh. I saw Gustavo help Jackie put away the blocks.) Typically, it takes several times before all children catch on and contribute. Let anyone who wishes to pass do so.
6. After going around the circle, say: "Pretzels is over." This signals the end of this part of a family meeting or a preschool "Pretzels" session.

7. Do not continue talking about comments made within the circle. Invite children to eat the pretzels, if they wish. Some may choose to save them as a reminder of others' affirmations.

In this ritual of giving, children learn how their actions affect others. They become aware of caring traits and can reflect on them. They can feel good about positive behavior and practice it in future interactions. They can see concrete evidence of their actions in the number of pretzels received at the close of the circle. In the end, young children go their separate ways, all a bit wiser.

Community Helpers

Point out to a young child plenty of community helpers who can inspire and make the preschooler feel more secure. Take advantage of special events when the child can interact with them. Perhaps you can visit the fire station during an open house when firefighters demonstrate equipment and offer children rides in the fire trucks. Introduce children to members of the canine corps or equestrian corps in urban police departments. Participate in or watch a bike safety event as children practice their own version of the rules of the road.

Encourage dramatic play, providing props that let preschoolers imagine themselves in situations that call for bravery, strength, patience, special skills, and caring behavior. If the child shows an avid interest in one particular role, support that interest with special activities, encounters with people already in that role, related books, and puppets or costumes that represent the police officer, doctor, or mail carrier. (See "Resources" on page 224 for information on where to find such props, puppets, and pretend uniforms.)

Role Models

If we were to ask preschoolers we know for a list of special people in their lives and why they like them, printing each name and each reason on a big yellow star like Officer Buckle's, how many shining role models would there be? In one community where we lived, preschoolers trembled at the thought of retrieving a rolling ball from the lawn of a persnickety neighbor. However, in another community, I once witnessed a front-yard kickball game for which the mom had supplied her living room sofa cushions for bases! Most folks fall somewhere in between

SAFETY FIRST

Providing supervision wherever our children find themselves, most adults think "safety first" and act accordingly. This is the motto of water safety instructors. It's at the top of the list when it comes to assessing the worthiness of a child-care site or preschool. It's the thought that drives us to childproof our homes and to carefully pick play groups, since we must trust others, too, to keep our children from harm.

We carry in our heads and in our hearts those true stories of events gone awry. Even the close calls make us nervous—that 4-year-old who called 911 when his grandma, caring for him, blacked out during a heart attack. It's enough to make you want to wallpaper a room with Officer Buckle's stars, forcing children to repeat the tips like mantras:

*   Never take other people's medicine.
*   Never put anything in your nose or ears.
*   Never play with the microwave oven.

Keep in mind, though, that while preschoolers can sometimes memorize a short list of rules, they cannot always put those guidelines into practice. It's not enough to introduce preschoolers to safety tips. They require appropriate supervision at all times, and gentle, or even stern, reminders when necessary. Impossible as the task may sometimes seem, all adults must assume the final responsibility for watching vigilantly over the children in their care.

on this continuum of caring. Adults can bring magic into a child's life with the simplest gifts of affection and attention.

Recruit a "rocking reader" to come in to read aloud to individual children in a classroom rocking chair. Reach out to a young child who is at risk for future failure. Supply someone who knows *your* child with a few concrete suggestions like the ones that follow. Depending on the circumstances and the relationship, an adult and child might:

*   Create a special handshake, a certain knock, a password, or pet names for each other.
*   Cook or bake something simple for a special event or in a certain season.
*   Start or add to the child's collection of stones, shells, plastic dinosaurs, finger puppets, stamps, costumes, funny hats, picture postcards, foreign coins, or silly jokes.
*   Share, if only in a small way, in the adult's favorite hobby or pastime— filling the bird feeder, visiting the farmers' market, taking photographs, looking at catalogs.
*   Remember birthdays (half-birthdays, too) with cards sent in the mail, small surprises, or books.
*   Take opportunities to discuss what a child is discovering about the world.

Boundaries-&-Expectations Bonus Best Bets

· ·

- **D. W. the Picky Eater** by Marc Brown. Boston: Little, Brown, 1995.

- **Fireman Small** by Wong Herbert Yee. Boston: Houghton Mifflin, 1994.

- **Harriet, You'll Drive Me Wild!** by Mem Fox. San Diego: Harcourt, 2000.

- **The Runaway Bunny** by Margaret Wise Brown. New York: HarperFestival, 2001 (oversize board book edition).

- **The Tale of Peter Rabbit** by Beatrix Potter. London: Frederick Warne, 1902, 1987 (original and authorized edition).

- **Voyage to the Bunny Planet (First Tomato, Moss Pillows, and The Island Light)** by Rosemary Wells. New York: Dial Books for Young Readers, 1992.

- **We Can Do It!** by Laura Dwight. New York: Star Bright Books, 1997.

Constructive Use of Time

OWL
MOON

by Jane Yolen

illustrated by John Schoenherr

How does the child in your life spend the time that holds unique potential for incredible growth? Does the preschooler dully pass the hours in places where there is little stimulation or engaging one-on-one interactions? Or, as this asset category implies, does he or she receive gifts that can include extended attention, creative activities, and exposure to spiritual experiences? Does the preschooler experience positive, supervised hours at home as well as out in the great wide world? Celebrating books, for example, represents time well spent.

• •

CHARACTERS IN ASSET-RICH BOOKS give grown-ups ideas of ways they can creatively and constructively spend time with children. They give young children a sense of others like them engaged in an ongoing and empowering discovery of the world.

Positive supervised time at home should include daily read-aloud encounters among the child's predictable, enjoyable routines. Books boost satisfaction with and understanding of the activities in which the child already takes part. They inspire new ways of doing. Books lend themselves to a host of creative follow-up activities. The toys you and the child relate to specific stories include hands-on materials (or literacy props) that call attention to print in our world. All are extensions of story.

Children, particularly those at highest risk, deserve to have access to books worth prizing and materials that promote language development. Is there a local service organization or business interested in bringing together young children and the best of books? Can you raise awareness of a need at a family literacy site, the nearby community center, or a shelter and raise funds through local businesses, congregations, or foundations to bring books to those in poverty and at high risk for future failure in school?

Owl Moon

. . . .

by Jane Yolen, illustrated by John Schoenherr. New York: Philomel Books, 1987.

VOTED THE BEST PICTURE BOOK OF 1987, this Caldecott Medal winner
has enchanted the many grown-ups and children who read about the
winter walk under a full moon. In it, a father and young child, hoping
to catch a glimpse of an owl, set off for an out-of-home stimulating
experience. Simple, poetic, quiet, this book also offers plenty of suspense and mystery. In a nighttime world, undetected creatures follow
the pair's progress, and a magnificent owl stuns everybody with its
appearance by story's end.

Before You Read Together

A child of undisclosed gender and a dad reach out toward each other
on a moonlit, snow-covered hillside, unaware of the shadowy shape
of the owl, in flight, on the back cover. Here's a promise that the owl
is out there somewhere, if only father and child are attentive enough
and quiet enough to hear it and spy it.

If your copy of this book—or one of the other winners featured in
these pages—boasts a shiny gold Caldecott Medal, you can tell the child
what it represents. Each year librarians choose, from thousands of con-
tenders, only one best picture book, with one or more runners-up or
honor books.

After You Read Aloud

- Invite the child to join in on the owl hoots when you read the
  story again. Naturalists say the rhythmic pattern sounds like
  "Who's awake? Me too!"
- Author Jane Yolen reveals on the dedication page that her husband took every one of their children "owling." Storytellers often

mix true events that have happened in their own lives with things that they make up. Ask the child if she's ever dictated or told such a story to you, mixing what has actually happened with what she wished could happen or what he knows couldn't happen. Express how glad you are that he has such a good imagination.

Owl Magic and Nighttime Wonder

Owl Moon inspired our family to take a night walk with a guide while vacationing along Lake Superior. We didn't sight an owl on that hike. Nonetheless it was a memorable event for kids who found being out and about in the pitch dark both daunting and delicious. A few years later, we moved to a house bordered by woods and have since seen our share of awe-inspiring owls. A barred owl, in particular, had unerring aim, nabbing—on breathtaking dives—mice, moles, and squirrels, all ingested on a favorite branch within view.

* At night, walk near woods, wetlands, deserts, or urban parks. In winter such a walk is most likely to yield a sighting (or hearing) of a great horned owl, featured in this story. They're the common big owls of North America, big enough to capture prey such as domestic cats, porcupines, and Canada geese!

* Colorful photographs of owls, along with brief descriptions, make the National Audubon Society pocket guide entitled *North American Birds of Prey* a helpful resource for identifying owls you see and appreciating their differences—from hoots to markings.

* Find out if there is a raptor center near you. These organizations often practice outreach, visiting schools and centers for educational purposes. Periodically they schedule public events for releasing birds of prey back into the wild.

* Fascinated by birds in general? View the video *Winged Migration* with the child, and, from the comfort of your armchair, fly with flocks as they migrate over the earth.

* Perhaps it's the hike itself, under a full moon, that captures the imagination of the child. If this is the case, set out when the moon is full any month of the year. September and October are especially beautiful for moonlit hikes, but springtime treks near marshes or other bodies of water expose children to the wondrous mating calls of tree frogs.

* Bring a flashlight. Covering it with a piece of red transparent cellophane or plastic wrap makes the light less unsettling to the critters you hope to encounter.
* Take necessary safety precautions, heeding, for instance, local warnings about predatory animals and ensuring that you don't become lost. Lather up with insect repellent in summer and wear long pants and sleeves. Dress warmly to deal with nighttime drops in temperature. Prepare preschoolers in advance with a recording of nature's night sounds, extended talk about the coming excursion, and a realistic plan that takes into account their age and attention spans.

Walking Poems

The natural impulse of children to put words together in unconventional ways has always bowled me over as both parent and teacher. I call kids "walking poems." Young children are especially unselfconscious about the poetic use of language. Maybe that's why they appreciate so much the metaphors and similes in *Owl Moon.* In any case, these phrases reverberate and resurface at other points in children's lives, enriching how they experience an event. Consider some of the lines the young listener can steep in the heart:

* *a train whistle blew / long and low, / like a sad, sad song*
* *my short, round shadow bumped after me*
* *I could feel the cold, / as if someone's icy hand / was palm-down on my back*
* *snow below it [the moon] was whiter than milk in a cereal bowl*

It is mesmerizing language, even when children are not quite sure what a more complex image (*the kind of hope that flies on silent wings*) means at this stage. They get the essence of the story. They feel their way through it with sensory images (*"My mouth felt furry, / for the scarf over it / was wet and warm"*). It helps them to make their own comparisons, with your encouragement, as you wonder together if the light on that water doesn't look like sparkling diamonds, if the tree outside your window isn't a wrinkled old man, if the tall glass building isn't like a giant tissue box. You notice wordplay and affirm it in your walking poem.

Friend-Trees

In the drama that plays out as these characters go owling, the trees serve as a memorable supporting cast. Take in their shapes and shadows to see if you don't find them almost as arresting as the sought-after owl. The text reads that *trees stood still / as giant statues* and yet, as they frame the grown-up and child, along with the hidden creatures, they seem alive to what is happening, very much a part of the magic.

* Introduce the child to friend-trees. Adopt a tree in the neighborhood. Pay special attention to one in particular and note how it changes through the four seasons. You and the preschooler can each draw it as you see it change. Hug it in loving greeting. Press or do a crayon rubbing of a few of its leaves. Picnic in its shade. Notice birds and animals that rest on its branches.

* If you have a yard, plant a tree in it. Let your child help return soil to the hole and to water it. Take a picture of your child standing next to it at the same time each year. Watch the tree and the child grow upward together. Host a party in honor of a tree. Draw pictures of and for it.

* Stretch a hammock between two trees and look up. Let the sound of leaves in the breeze lull both of you to sleep.

* Hang a bird feeder or birdhouse in a tree on your property. If you have access to a small deciduous tree that has died, bring the tree inside, anchor it in plaster of Paris in a basket or pot, and hang whimsical objects from its branches. (A beloved birch graces a corner of our den with painted fish suspended from its branches.) A child might like to have a small bare tree in a pot on which to hang brightly colored buttons, origami birds, painted wooden hearts, hole-punched photos of favorite people (a *family* tree), or homemade ornaments.

* Visit a nature center or an arboretum to experience natural habitat where trees are the main event. Take in the sounds of wind in the leaves and birds chirping. Wander and wonder.

Jingle Dancer

● ●

by Cynthia Leitich Smith, illustrated by Cornelius Van Wright and Ying-Hwa Hu.
New York: Morrow Junior Books, 2000.

JENNA IS A PRESENT-DAY MEMBER of the Muscogee, or Creek Nation (she
is also, as the author's note tells us, of Ojibway descent). She borrows
jingles from the dresses of various older family members and friends to
perform her first jingle dance at a powwow. This main character, a few
years older than preschoolers, has been waiting to participate in the
dance she has seen her grandmother and other relatives perform. As in
Where Did You Get Your Moccasins? by Bernelda Wheeler, *Jingle Dancer*
features Native American characters living contemporary lives who also
honor their past—in this case, with traditional clothes, dances, and foods
at a celebration. The child anticipates an asset-enriching event that
allows for self-expression, physical activity, and interaction with others.

Before You Read Together

The main character, beaming and waving aloft her eagle feathers, wears
ornaments on her dress that the child may guess are the jingles mentioned in the title. In the background, dancing grown-ups in colorful
traditional dress make it obvious that this girl will be part of an exciting
performance or celebration. A few words on the back cover introduce
the plot, the challenge, and, possibly, new words, such as *powwow* and
jingles, to explain to your child before reading.

After You Read Aloud

- Native American practices and perspectives, even manners
  of speech, as when an article like *the* is dropped (e.g., "Jenna
  bounce-stepped on family room carpet"), make this worthy of
  exploration together if these elements are unfamiliar to you.
  Talk about how a dress could "lose its voice" or how "Sun caught
  a glimpse of Moon."

Exploring Sound

Let this story about a child embracing the rhythms, music, movement, and customs of her forebears and family inspire you and your growing child to listen up—and boogie! Make him proud to recognize all the dimensions of sound.

* Let the preschooler know that *percussion* instruments require hitting or striking two parts together to make sound. Experiment, making sounds that are loud and soft, fast and slow.

* Find a small plastic storage container or a box with a lid. Take turns filling it one-quarter to one-half full with different types of materials. First try rice, birdseed, or uncooked beans. Next, try pebbles, then jingle bells, and paper clips, perhaps. Shake to discover the sound each type of item makes. Let the child choose a favorite sound or material and return it to the container. Tape the lid shut, and add it to a collection of rhythm instruments.

* Beat a drum or tambourine. In 4/4 time—with four beats or quarter notes of equal length in each measure or set—make each first beat louder. Have the child copy your rhythm on any of a range of household drums—a cookie tin, an empty oatmeal container, a pot, or a plastic bowl fitted with a waxed paper cover secured with a rubber band. Move to the beat, marching or dancing. Next, try three short beats and then one long one, repeating this over and over. Ask the child to come up with a pattern you both can play.

* Use a drum, a tambourine, a homemade shaker, or two rhythm sticks (shortened dowels, sanded for safety) and accompany the music you hear on tapes, CDs, or the radio.

* Occasionally, stop to listen to and identify every sound you hear together. Is there rhythm or a pattern in some noises? Can the child mimic any of them?

* Take inspiration from the jingle dancer of the story. Measure a band of felt the length of the child's wrist (or ankle). Then secure Velcro to one end of the top side of the fabric and more Velcro at the other end of the underside. Sew on four or five jingle bells in a row. Borrow from the library a recording of powwow dance rhythms and let the child jingle and move to the music.

Rhythm and Repetition

Let the child's gift for absorbing and delighting in almost anything be reason enough to branch out from familiar genres to music of people from all over the planet.

* For a great source of world music, try the public library or record stores.
* Be open when it comes to listening. Jazz, blues, bluegrass, zydeco, gospel—virtually anything goes, though it's important to let the child decide what he likes and wants to listen to again.
* Age-appropriate children's music can be lots of fun. (For a few suggested sources of this music, see "Resources" on page 224.)
* Count on folk songs and lullabies, including those sung in another language, to prompt the child to sing along. The way these old favorites incorporate refrains, recurring phrases, or repeated melodies makes them easy and fun for young children to master.
* React with delight and interest whenever the child creates a variation of an existing song or sings something entirely new. But keep in mind that wild praise may create performance anxiety. Simple comments, such as "I like the words you're singing," "That tune is catchy," or "What a happy song!" provide support for play but don't demand a finished product.
* Encourage the child to chant simple words along with you or to invent a tune for rhymes.
* Teach the preschooler how to operate a simple tape recorder or CD player so that he can listen to favorite selections at will. Recurring encounters with music expand the repertoire of songs she knows by heart. It's a terrific way to build vocabulary.
* Invite the child to fingerpaint to certain musical selections, mimicking the tempo.

Creative Movement

Here's the part of a preschooler's musical education that requires you to walk on the wild side. I'm addressing anybody who has two left feet, anybody who never learned to do the twist or the cha-cha. A klutz on the dance floor, I still "dance" in the privacy of my own home. Doing so in the company of a child of 5 or younger is heaven on earth. Just think, a partner who does not judge, who only takes joy. What are you waiting for?

* Make thoughtful selections if the child wants to play along with rhythm instruments or move for any length of time. Even so-called kids' music can be too fast.
* This is not about teaching the steps of a waltz or a polka. Merely suggest a simple pattern or a particular way to slither or twirl.
* Use books for inspiration. To *Jingle Dancer,* add Eric Carle's *From Head to Toe,* George Ancona's *Let's Dance!,* Jean Marzollo's *Pretend You're a Cat,* José-Luis Orozco's *Diez Deditos* or *De Colores and Other Latin-American Folk Songs for Children,* Harriet Zeifert's *Animal Music,* and Brian Pinkney's *Max Found Two Sticks.*
* Sew jingle bells to a shirt or skirt hem. Provide scarves or boas to add pizzazz to every sweep and turn.
* The best way to motivate the child is to show that you enjoy music and movement. However, if the child is reluctant to dance, let her play an instrument along with a tape. Introduce musical or rhythm instruments one by one, providing time for guided discovery of each one's shape, color, parts, and sound along with the proper way to play it.

A Child's Calendar

• •

by John Updike, illustrated by Trina Schart Hyman. New York: Holiday House, 1999.

THE 12 POEMS in this Caldecott Honor winner describe seasonal activities in a child's life as the year moves from January to December. Poems especially warrant second and third readings. Young children will ponder the rich metaphors and similes (*Frost bites the lawn. / The stars are slits / In a black cat's eye / Before it spits*). Some may ask for explanations; others will be content to revel in the language's "music" and mystery, with understanding to come gradually with experience. Detailed illustrations also provide many examples of constructive use of time.

Before You Read Together

On the dust jacket, two young children with sleds survey a hill. On the back of the jacket are single symbols for corresponding months (a heart, a kite, a flag, a leafless tree) interspersed with kids of different ages, including a toddler. Talk with your preschooler. Does she have a grasp of special occasions, holidays, or activities that help her define the months? If your child has had exposure to a calendar, the title hints at what's in store.

After You Read Aloud

- Approach this beautiful book in a variety of ways. At first, take in the illustrated seasonal activities without reading a line. The picture of a little one studying chickadees at a feeder may prompt discussion about your child's similar experience. She may enjoy spying pets on as many pages as possible. One image in particular may prompt a request for you to read a poem.

- Invite the preschooler to echo a word or line that pleases. It can provide new ways of seeing an everyday event. In March, one may have an "Aha!" moment, remembering the phrase "the mud smells happy on our shoes" or, in April, "the sky's a herd of prancing sheep."

Serendipity Days

What does a typical month on your calendar look like? In addition to scheduled child-care arrangements and learning opportunities, is there a place for plain old TV-free relaxation, for ritual? Do you make the time to be mindfully present for your preschooler and other children in your life? Can you "X" out a day or a half-day each month for your preschooler that holds no commitments, such as haircut appointments, T-ball games, and supermarket shopping? Can you save that time for something you and the child agree would be a great way to use her (and your) *present?*

When our children were school-age, they celebrated Serendipity Days each year. With advance notice of at least two days or more (so that one or both parents could participate), each child separately called a halt to business as usual. Once a year, each opted not to go to school. (They liked school; nonetheless, they found the privilege not to show up one day out of the school year both exciting and empowering.) They were invariably resourceful about how they chose to use the gift of unscheduled hours—grown-up and child balancing excursions with quiet time for simply enjoying each other's company.

Care providers and preschool teachers can indulge in a bit of serendipity, too, by mixing things up. Try following the familiar schedule backward, promise surprise visitors and activities on a certain day each month, or celebrate with a specific theme, such as pretend travel. Create a make-believe luau in Hawaii, an undersea setting, or an imaginary, letter-filled Alphabet City.

On the last day of each month, take a peek at where you've been and where you're going, consulting that symbolic grid called the *calendar.* Point out for your preschooler coming events, not only the holidays that a preschool teacher or care provider may highlight, but also family birthdays, special occasions, and, if the spirit moves you, a square reserved just for serendipity—with your child calling the shots.

Wiggly Magic

Invite your preschooler to contribute an item to a special meal or a midday snack. Here's a simple recipe that's adaptable for different events, as long as you have one or more cookie cutters related to the occasion and gelatin of the color associated with it. You can make it well in advance. The adult should handle the boiling and adding of water.

MAGIC FINGER GELATIN

2 packets of unflavored gelatin

One 6-ounce box (or two 3-ounce boxes) of flavored gelatin in a flavor/color associated with a holiday

2 1/2 cups water

1/4 cup or less of sugar

1. Dissolve unflavored gelatin in one cup of cold water. Set aside.
2. Bring one cup of water to a boil in a saucepan and add the box(es) of flavored gelatin and sugar.
3. Once the mixture has come to a boil, remove it from the heat with care.
4. Add the unflavored gelatin-and-water mixture. Stir and add 1/2 cup of COLD water.
5. Pour all into a greased 9-x-9-inch pan. Set in the refrigerator until solid (about 2 hours).

Later, using cookie cutters, cut into shapes associated with the appropriate holiday: cherry or strawberry heart shapes on Valentine's Day, lime green shamrocks for St. Patrick's Day, or orange pumpkin shapes at Halloween. With other cookie cutters, you can make geometric shapes, alphabet letters, or numbers. Another option: Cut the gelatin into 1- or 1½-inch squares when introducing or practicing the use of child-size chopsticks. Store any of these shapes in an airtight container in the refrigerator until serving.

"Happy" Boxes

My friend Mary endorses this delightful and doable way to record highlights of a child's year: keep a small container with a lid, such as a recipe box, filled with index cards for notations. You may wish to add a set of dividers labeling the 12 months.

At bedtime or at the end of the child-care stay, briefly talk about the day's experiences. Let the preschooler decide whether the highlight was the sighting of a raccoon, a visit from a favorite uncle, or good feelings about staying upright on skates. Jot down this comment and, if you wish, add a highlight of your own. This ritual allows for one-on-one time and, used as a daily or weekly ritual, provides an easy way to record history as the child lives it.

A variation on this theme is a box for belongings that signify for your child important milestones, memorable experiences, and everyday sources of wonder. In this special box, encourage him to accumulate mementos of times that have made him happiest. On days when he is feeling down in the dumps, take several minutes to go through the small treasures and remember together the best of times. Eventually your child may turn independently to this activity as a way to restore inner calm or generate good feelings through recollection.

Give shelf space to a container for items associated with different holidays, special occasions, and seasons, a source for enrichment especially useful for group settings. Play a game, challenging a preschooler to recall the names of activities or seasons associated with items that you retrieve, one by one, from the box—a Halloween mask, a mitten, a birthday candle, a packet of seeds.

Hurray for Pre-K!

• •

by Ellen B. Senisi. New York: HarperCollins, 2000.

THIS PHOTOGRAPHIC TOUR of an early childhood classroom features real children and grown-ups interacting with each other as they move through a day. Engaging experiences with a variety of age-appropriate materials occur in this out-of-home program staffed with competent adults. It's just what's needed, according to the asset framework, to ensure constructive and creative use of time in the community.

Before You Read Together

Ask your child how one knows this classroom is a happy place to be. The covers give lots of clues: kids and grown-ups are smiling and hugging. Children reach out with a friendly touch. The title itself shouts *Hurray!*—a word of gladness and celebration. On the back, many inviting materials compete for attention, but at center stage is a group of preschoolers enjoying a hands-on activity. Just inside, the endpapers show the children's colorful and free-spirited artwork.

After You Read Aloud

- Key words in the text illustrate important features of any young child's day. Each verb calls attention to itself in three different ways: (1) the word appears in big black letters; (2) the word, used in a sentence, shows up in a bright contrasting color; and (3) the word appears three times between a repeating photo that illustrates its meaning. Encourage the prereader to notice that a word's shape and sequence of letters remain the same, even when the size or color changes. After multiple readings, a child may begin to recognize certain words on sight.

- Look at the key verbs displayed on the final pages. Talk about each. Does the preschooler understand their meanings? Visualize how the child (or children) in your life actually hears and uses each one, whether paying attention (listening) or learning chants and songs (singing). How can you add to or enrich any of these vocabulary experiences in the preschooler's day?

Finger Painting Fun

Find a washable, nonporous surface such as Formica or create one, covering a surface with plastic sheeting, a piece of oilcloth, or contact paper. Roll up your sleeves (and everybody else's) and get ready for visual and tactile surprises that come with shaving cream art! Using an aerosol can of shaving cream, put a large dollop on the surface in front of the painter. Encourage the preschooler to:

- Enjoy finger play as he mashes it between fingers and palms and then onto the table.
- Press and move one or more fingers deeply enough for the colored surface to show through the shaving cream in order to make a picture or design of one's choosing.
- Follow the grown-up's example, if desired, and make a repeating pattern. Depending on the child's level of eye-hand coordination, let her copy your step-by-step creation of simple forms (a wiggly line, a straight line, a rectangle) or simple letters (F, L, O, T). Make sure to name or identify the shape or letter. The child may wish to experiment with other shapes.
- To start over, gently swipe a palm across the surface and add more cream, if needed. Celebrate the ease with which shaving cream cleans up, disappearing like magic after applying a wash-cloth and water.

A popular alternative is to substitute instant chocolate pudding mix, blended according to package directions. Follow the procedure described above for artwork done "in good taste"—with as much bonus tasting as the artist wishes.

The Wish List

Some see kid-space like the one in *Hurray for Pre-K!* and feel over-whelmed. They decide that theirs can never measure up. Others begin immediately to "dwell in possibility." They brainstorm ways to overcome what others see as a pitiful lack of funds or support. For me, this possibility thinking begins with taking time to make a wish list. I've found that identifying what one wants and needs, then putting it in black and white, plays a powerful part in prompting the universe to respond. Whether I've scribbled my own private list for enrichment on the home front, listed wishes for supplies on a classroom blackboard during open house, or relayed the list to people in the community on behalf of an out-of-home program, the results have been amazing. What do you wish for? Follow these ideas to turn those wishes into reality:

* Engage in positive thinking. Examine your thoughts. Reject a can't-be-done attitude. Adults who get accustomed to doubting a positive outcome model this attitude for children who witness and absorb adults' approach to challenges, to life.
* Prioritize. Zero in on three to five items, activities, or resources you wish could be part of daily experience for the preschoolers in your life. Visualize these in place.
* Put your wish list in print. Put it out there. Post it where you and others can see it.
* Pick a potential partner or partners. Think of several people, agencies, businesses, and/or service organizations that might honor your wish and offer support—as cheerleaders, networking links, or contributors.
* Participate in the process. Look and listen. Rich Aunt Tallulah and Bill Gates are not the only sources of fulfillment in the world. Situations and encounters often occur that hold the seeds to getting the results you've wished for.
* Trust in abundance. Believe in your worthiness to receive it. When you achieve your wishes, give thanks. And model for children that there's enough good to go around.

TV or Not TV . . . ?

Wonder of wonders, the children in this book spend not a single moment in front of a TV screen, reflecting an asset that recommends minimal TV viewing. A nationwide study revealed that while centers often lack for high-quality books and story times, TVs are usually part of the landscape—this despite evidence about the negative effects on young children of watching most TV programming. Is television center stage in your child-care setting or at home?

Studies show that preschool-age children who watch cartoons or other shows and videos designed solely for entertainment do poorer than their peers on prereading skills. At a critical stage for brain development, viewing between ages 3 and 5 takes the place of verbal interactions and stimulating activities. Researchers have found that children between 2 and 17 spend more time watching TV than on any activity other than sleeping—on average, almost 25 hours of television per week.

I asked David Walsh, Ph.D., founder and president of the National Institute on Media and the Family (www.mediafamily.org), to cite five important tips for caregivers of the preschool set:

1. Keep television and video games out of kids' bedrooms.
2. Take care that babies 2 years and under have very limited exposure to television and videos.
3. In accordance with recommendations from the American Academy of Pediatrics, expose preschoolers to no more than one to two hours of nonviolent age-appropriate TV programming, videos, and video games per day.
4. Select TV programs, such as *Sesame Street,* and videos that encourage prereading skills.
5. Always know what the children are watching.

In Every Tiny Grain of Sand: A Child's Book of Prayers and Praise

• •

by Reeve Lindbergh (compiler), illustrated by Christine Davenier, Bob Graham, Anita Jeram, and Elisa Kleven. Cambridge, MA: Candlewick Press, 2000.

HERE ARE 77 PRAYERS AND POEMS, from many cultures and faiths around the world, in four sections: "For the Day," "For the Home," "For the Earth," and "For the Night." Popular artists from four countries provide the exuberant illustrations. The selections offer "young children and families of all beliefs the gifts of deeply felt tradition, abiding comfort, and spiritual strength." A resource to enrich family life, this book links to the Developmental Assets framework, supporting age-appropriate spiritual activities that reflect a family's beliefs—building feelings of security, optimism, and caring for others.

Before You Read Together

This offering initially may seem imposing. The day may come, however, when you realize it has become the oft-used and prized possession. Talk about the cover as always. Mention that instead of collecting stones or toy figures, a person collected favorite prayers and poems and put them in a book.

After You Read Aloud

- Let the child lead, sampling the succession of pictures only, or hearing one favorite poem repeatedly, or listening to several selections at random.
- To create a ritual, introduce a "keeper" at meal or snack time or a simple poem to start or end your time together.

- Read a longer poem in lieu of a lullaby as the child falls asleep.
- Incorporate just a portion of a poem into everyday exchanges—
  "Hurt no living thing," for example, when you encounter a spider
  or ants.

Giving Thanks

I'll never forget the sight of two long tables of young children at pre-school, my 3-year-old daughter one of them, about to savor a mid-morning snack. In the blink of an eye, every one of them folded their hands and recited, as one, words they had already steeped in the heart: "We wish food, peace, and happiness for all the children of the world."

My heart did a flip-flop. Theirs was not, technically, a prayer of thanks—perhaps not a prayer at all. Yet rolled into the wish, this decep-tively simple plea, was acknowledgment of the food before them and the reasonable amounts of peace and happiness that they already claimed. Here was an honoring of the truth that these precious gifts are *every* child's due. I was struck by how the simple daily ritual could shape a child's worldview and make generosity of spirit and appreciation of *every* human being as much a *given* as juice and crackers. All this in a single moment of attention and appreciation.

As part of the fabric of our children's days, a simple line or two is not a small thing to offer. Collections such as Lindbergh's or *A Child's Book of Blessings* by Sabrina Dearborn or *Blessings and Prayers for Little Bears* by Linda Hill Griffith provide the source material for pausing and proclaiming our thanks, prayers, and wishes. Whether or not your family participates in a religious tradition, there are forms of thanksgiving that you and your child can create and express. On the quest for what reso-nates in your hearts, consider sharing expressions such as the following:

> The bread is pure and fresh,
> The water cool and clear.
> Lord of all life, be with us,
> Lord of all life, be near.
>   —African prayer

> For all that has been, Thanks.
> For all that will be, Yes.
>   —Dag Hammarskjöld

Houses of Worship

Studies show that churches, mosques, and synagogues are prime places to build assets. They remain among the few institutions that sustain intergenerational community. Wise elders cross paths with careening toddlers, young and old sit side by side—or could, with a bit of encouragement. Faith communities provide children a chance for sustained relationships outside the immediate family and over time. Parents who find themselves loyal to or drawn back into religious communities may do so not only for spiritual sustenance but also for the wellspring of support that helps their family to thrive.

Rituals seem to figure in whenever people introduce Spirit into their lives. In a book by Synthia Saint James called *Sunday*, now out of print, an African American family spends a portion of the day celebrating the walk to church, the weekly reunion with Grandma and Grandpa, the preacher's sermon, the joyful voices of the choir, and visits "with friends big and small." They practice other rituals faithfully as well, such as eating a breakfast of pancakes piled high and traveling to the grandparents' house, where they listen to stories and, before supper, give thanks. These rituals also transform an ordinary day into sacred time each week.

My friend Andy asserts that the best "church" is the great outdoors. Here is where he feels most keenly the presence of Spirit. I think it interesting that in this anthology, the four illustrators happen to show children in virtually every picture celebrating life outdoors.

Anywhere we experience the soulful or the transcendent—in a church, mosque, temple, home, or stand of trees—qualifies as a house of worship. In each place, we can give thanks. We can create meaningful rituals with others of different ages. We can appreciate the miraculous unfolding of creation and give to children a sense of time and place as holy.

Poetry's Power

The music in words becomes a source of delight. Referring to Gerard Manley Hopkins's poem "Pied Beauty," which her sister once recited to her, Lindbergh admits in her foreword: "I still don't know what a brindled cow is, exactly, but I can feel the glory of creation, in a simple way that makes sense, whenever I read that poem."

Oft-repeated poems turn young children into "experts," able to predict the rhyming word or the completing phrase, even if meaning eludes them. They devour this satisfying stew of syllables and become more and more adept at discerning the separate ingredients, individual sounds tripping over the tongue.

I've had such an experience, listening to an audio version of the book *Diez Deditos,* sung by José-Luis Orozco. I don't understand Spanish, but, by the third hearing, I found myself happily joining in on verses, delighting in the combinations of sounds themselves.

To this collection of poetry, add others such as Josette Frank's *Poems to Read to the Very Young.* Graduate to another treasure trove: *Talking Like the Rain: A Read-to-Me Book of Poems* selected by X. J. Kennedy and Dorothy M. Kennedy. Relate a handful to a special interest. Pluck one or two prior to reading picture books. Read each twice, savoring new ways of looking at something. Absorb the "music." Introduce the child to poetry's pleasures and power.

Constructive-Use-of-Time Bonus Best Bets

• •

- **Father Fox's Pennyrhymes** by Clyde Watson, illustrated by Wendy Watson. New York: HarperCollins, 2001.

- **Max Found Two Sticks** by Brian Pinkney. New York: Simon & Schuster Books for Young Readers, 1994.

- **Peter Spier's Rain** by Peter Spier. Garden City, NY: Bantam Doubleday Dell Books for Young Readers, 1997.

- **Pretend You're a Cat** by Jean Marzollo, illustrated by Jerry Pinkney. New York: Puffin Pied Piper/Penguin, 1997.

- **Stella and Roy Go Camping** by Ashley Wolff. New York: Dutton Children's Books, 1999.

- **A Summery Saturday Morning** by Margaret Mahy. New York: Viking, 1998.

- **Sunday** by Synthia Saint James. Morton Grove, IL: Albert Whitman, 1996.

Commitment to Learning

The Jamie and Angus Stories

Anne Fine

illustrated by Penny Dale

To get schooled in what makes learning such an ongoing pleasure, a child doesn't need to be school age. In fact, caring grownups shape the attitude the child carries to kindergarten. A child whose life is filled with reading for pleasure and book ownership is fortunate indeed. Exposure to stimulating toys, age-appropriate materials, and activities like ones suggested here enhance the joy of learning. Most important is the attitude toward learning that adults exude. All combine to make a young human being ready—rather than reticent or resistant—to learn.

THE ASSETS RELATED TO A COMMITMENT TO LEARNING—particularly asset 25, early literacy—represent the most obvious link between building assets and raising readers. Daily bonding with the best of books provides necessary brain stimulation during a period of tremendous growth. The most stimulating content—shown to boost readiness skills—includes rhyming words, alliteration, repetition and predictable word patterns, songs, finger plays and chants, and humorous or ingenious wordplay.

The books featured in *Playful Reading* have garnered praise as exceptionally fine children's literature. Each selection has the added advantage of beautifully reflecting a portion of one or more asset categories. A loving grown-up introduces the books. A child subsequently may seek out any of them for independent enjoyment. In either case, the story content and the context in which the pleasurable reading experience occurs both contribute to asset enrichment, to helping a young life flourish.

Let's be clear about this: Teaching preschoolers how to decode print for meaning (i.e., to actually read the words) is developmentally inappropriate. On the other hand, opportunities abound in any read-aloud session for naturally and informally building vocabulary and phonemic awareness (the ability to distinguish differences between sounds). It is this kind of learning that begins long before kindergarten.

Wemberly Worried

· ·

by Kevin Henkes. New York: Greenwillow Books/HarperCollins, 2000.

KEVIN HENKES'S BOOKS are popular with preschoolers, perhaps because they are populated with endearing mice who meet challenges not unlike the ones young children face. There's Owen, who refuses to go off to school without his blanket, and Julius—"the baby of the world"—whose sister wishes, initially, that he would disappear. Lily can't wait for show-and-tell time and doesn't. Chided by her teacher for disobeying the rules, she draws a picture of him that requires an apology. In this book, Wemberly worries about life in general—odd noises, potentially widening wall cracks, possibly loose bolts on the playground slide—and, in particular, her first day of nursery school. But don't worry—there's a happy ending.

As the Developmental Assets framework reveals, by helping a child feel positive about experiences in out-of-home and educational programs, adults make sure that a preschooler, after an initial period of adjustment, attends willingly.

Before You Read Together

Ears pricked, eyes wide open, looking out in alarm, with a toy clutched in her arms, Wemberly *does* look worried. After looking at the cover together, ask the child what in the world could be worrying Wemberly. Then ask if some of those guesses include things the preschooler sometimes worries about. Can you reassure her? Can you acknowledge that sometimes worrying helps to prepare us for the unexpected and sometimes it just makes things harder?

After You Read Aloud

- Think back to times when each of you worried about something that proved to be nothing to fret about. Share your recollections.
- Clap out the syllables in Wemberly's name (1-2-3). Clap out the ones in the child's name and your name. Invite the child to clap, too. Print Wemberly's name and, in same-size letters, yours above it. Add a one-syllable name below it. Does the child see that names (and other words) that use more sounds (or claps) also use more letters and take up more space on paper? See if the child can come up with a long word and a short word. Print those for comparison.
- Reserve time after each read-aloud session for discussion as the child makes comments, expresses feelings, and asks questions about her coming experience in preschool or kindergarten.

Feeling at Home out of Home

It's important for adults—parents, child-care providers, teachers—to collaborate in easing the transitions a child experiences. This mutual concern drives their efforts. Here are recommendations from a variety of experts in child development:

- If possible, together visit the caregiver or teacher and the new setting in advance.
- Prepare your child by talking about the feelings that accompany being away: "We will miss each other during the day. Your teacher will be there to care for you. I'll like hearing all about what fun things you did. I'll always come back for you."
- Allow your child to bring along, as Wemberly does, a transitional object—a beloved blanket, plush animal, or doll—to be a source of soothing comfort and a bridge to home. Another child may rely on a thumb to suck or an imaginary friend.
- If your child demonstrates a need for your presence, smooth the transition by delaying your departure, if possible.
- Assess and own up to your own feelings of anxiety and loss. Does your child sense your fears? Determine whether you or she is having a more difficult time with the separation. Wemberly may have picked up on her own parents' anxieties as well.

* Provide a "safety zone" for your child, accepting that he may let off steam or "behave badly" at pickup or at home. Carve out focused time for physical closeness and quiet talk as soon as you arrive at home, reestablishing your connection.
* Talk with the caregiver or teacher about any concerns. Visit and observe your child's interactions and activities, especially if you think her transition continues to be a challenging one.

"Guide" Books

Picture books are useful guides for preparing children for preschool or kindergarten. Read a number of ones about transitions. Expose the child to different characters' experiences so that he understands that settings and situations vary, but that each has in common group inter-actions, enjoyable activities, and nurturing caregivers. During the first weeks, a return visit to certain books provides a springboard to make comparisons, bring up concerns, and affirm the real-life experience.

Miriam Cohen's books, in a series that features a preschooler by the name of Jim, are among the best candidates. In each, she deftly captures a preschooler's point of view and deals with one aspect of the out-of-home experience. In fact, these serve children heading for kindergarten as well. A group of other excellent candidates follow, with "P" indicating a transition to a preschool-level setting and "K" indicat-ing a transition to kindergarten:

Adam's Daycare by Julie Ovenell-Carter (P) (Featured on page 12.)

Born in the Gravy by Denys Cazet (K)

Building a Bridge by Lisa Shook Begaye (K)

First Day by Dandi Daley Mackall (P or K)

Hurray for Pre-K! by Ellen B. Senisi (P) (Featured on page 93.)

Little School by Beth Norling (P)

Look Out Kindergarten, Here I Come! by Nancy Carlson
    (Spanish edition: *¡Prepárate, kindergarten! ¡Allá voy!*) (K)

My Kindergarten by Rosemary Wells (K)

Owen by Kevin Henkes (P)

Will I Have a Friend? by Miriam Cohen (P or K)

Art for Art's Sake

Moving toward the age of 5, preschoolers become more likely to compare the work or skills of others with their own. More aware of their peers, they may see their own creations in black-and-white terms. Like Jim in Miriam Cohen's *No Good in Art*, they can feel inadequate to a task.

Make your setting an encouraging and safe one for experimenting and taking artistic risks. Say, "Tell me about your drawing," rather than "What is it?" Comment in a matter-of-fact manner about specific details. Avoid comparisons between the work of siblings or friends. Make it clear that kids deserve gold stars for diving in, for daring to do something unique. Resist lockstep directions—"Now cut out the black hat and paste it over the snowman's head." Provide open-ended activities that allow for all kinds of expression. An example, Moving String Art, follows. You'll need:

- ☐ Large sheets of white paper
- ☐ Length of string (approximately 8 inches)
- ☐ Plastic drinking straw
- ☐ Black ink in a bottle
- ☐ Colored pastels or chalks
- ☐ Spray fixative (optional)

1. Spread a surface with newspaper or another protective material. Place a sheet of paper on top of it.
2. Tie one end of the string to one end of the plastic drinking straw. Have the child hold the opposite end of the straw and dip the string into the ink.
3. Lifting the ink-coated string out and still holding the stringless straw end, the child can move the string over any part of the paper and/or lightly shake the string above the paper.
4. Encourage her to experiment with light and dark, straight and curvy lines, as well as different hand movements above the paper. Let her continue to dip, drag, and dab until she's satisfied.
5. Repeat the process on one or more additional sheets, with lots of marks on some and few on others. He or she may "see" shapes and figures similar to ones spied in cloud formations.
6. When the ink dries, invite the artist to add colors to parts of the black-and-white forms or designs. Use spray fixative, if desired.

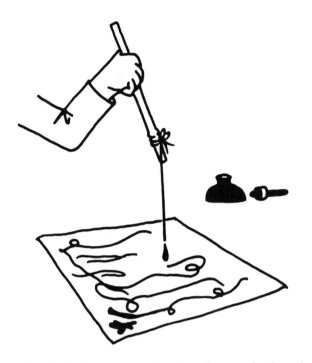

Alternatives include using paint and craft-store feathers instead of brushes, or cutting sponges into various shapes and dabbing them, dipped in different colors of paint, onto paper.

And If the Moon Could Talk

by Kate Banks, illustrated by Georg Hallensleben. New York: Frances Foster Books/Farrar, Straus & Giroux, 1998.

A CHILD MOVES FROM WAKEFULNESS TO DREAMS in the cozy, comfy world of her room as the moon outside her own window looks down on other places on the planet. As the author tells us, if the moon could talk, it would murmur a reassuring "Good night." Adult and child, bonding to book and to each other, show the rightful place of early literacy in a young life.

Before You Read Together

A child peeks over the edge of a quilt. A rabbit's tucked in beside the child. A moon hangs outside the window. Surely a little detective will figure out it's bedtime! Open the book to the endpapers just inside the covers. They reveal a moonlit town filled with houses glowing with light. Ask: "Does the child on the cover live in one of them?" Imagine together what's happening in this town before its children go to sleep.

After You Read Aloud

- If you or the child is a fan of the classic *Goodnight Moon* by Margaret Wise Brown, you may find elements in this story amusingly or amazingly similar. Talk about such similarities—a rabbit at bedtime, a red bed, a round moon presiding over everything, favorite belongings "inventoried" before sleep, and a peaceful sense that all is well.
- The child in the story absorbs what her father is reading aloud and then dreams a variation of its content. Ask if the preschooler in your life remembers any dreams. Does he realize that sometimes things we encounter in our waking hours can show up in our dream life?

- Here's an opportunity to talk with the child about what she likes and what she wishes were different about bedtime at home.

Just the Ticket!

At a very young age, my mother accompanied a friend on a first visit to the public library. The youngest of 12 children of immigrant parents, she was terrified that she would be carted off to jail for lack of a "ticket" like the one her friend flashed in front of the clerk in exchange for the beautiful books. Surely, this innocent child reasoned, these couldn't be free for the taking. Surely she was trespassing and apt to be caught any minute!

The beauty of the public library is that the treasure is free for the taking, intended for richer and for poorer. At the public library:

* Entertain a child at story time;
* Entice a preschooler with puppets, book-and-tape sets, and computer access;
* Empower a child to choose from a bounty of multilingual books;
* Enrich a child's choices with additional recommended reading of your choosing; and
* Enjoy the bounty later in the privacy of your own home or preschool room!

If you have no other reason for making the library a regular destination, consider this one: in *Access for All* (see "Acknowledgments" on page 225), the authors report that some experts recommend exposing preschoolers to at least 100 books each year. If, like most, you're not apt to pop for the lot, give thanks for the library loan. For families with obstacles like a lack of transportation or bus fare, demands of infant care or multiple jobs, and language-related or cultural barriers, dedicated people have brought the library to the child—using grant money to stock a lending library at the early childhood site or arranging for popular on-site visits of a library bookmobile.

In addition to regular library visits, every child deserves to connect with the kind of book that merits reading again and again: a *keeper*, bought for a birthday or holiday, using windfalls or spare change accumulating in the family "book" jar or the school's gift book budget; or a *winner* borrowed with a specific child's personality and interests in mind.

What to do with them all? Model gentle and respectful handling. Make sure they're within reach—that they whisper "come hither" in the home and in the classroom. Be sure to display the books on shelves at child-height, with covers facing forward. Then, if the books call "Open sesame!", the prereader *can*. If you're intent on raising readers, bringing a lending library into their world is just the ticket!

The Best Book in the World

A work authored by a preschooler is a book like no other. Invest in a scrapbook with blank pages or fold in half several sheets of paper and staple them together. Add pictures that serve as story starters. I glued greeting cards into the scrapbook, one to each page. Funny, intriguing, or exciting magazine pictures will do as well. Then every so often sit down with the 4- or 5-year-old and invite the storyteller to invent a story using one of the pictures for inspiration. In large print, take care to transcribe the narration word for word. Then read it back. Whenever you're asked, jot down a new story to go with a different illustration or return for a rereading of past creations.

When my son went off to college, he took along three links to early childhood:

* Boo Bear, a companion from his 6th month of life on, worn to the nub.
* A spiral-bound, photocopied collection of his artwork, from toddler scribbles to works he generated at the arts high school he attended.
* Last, but certainly not least, a scrapbook album called *Kai's Big Storybook*. In his 4th and 5th years, he had dictated each story to me or to his dad, and we'd printed them word for word.

Our 20-something son has admitted to returning to his storybook on numerous occasions, whenever he needs a laugh or a link to an age when almost everything was new. It's a time machine, he's told me — a bridge to his childhood, in general, and to his particular mental processes at the time.

Recalling the excitement of creating his own tales, he tells me:

At 4 years old, I was the world's greatest author. There was the wit I exercised in naming characters like "Dodo Corestio," the skill with which I molded their identities (Dodo Corestio can't get enough watermelon), and the care I took to direct their fates (Dodo is eaten by a shark). Move over, Oscar Wilde!

It still amazes him that this activity had any purpose other than pure fun. Encourage active participation in this learning experience, a novelty providing pleasure and success, just as the Developmental Assets framework recommends. The language-rich activity has long-lasting impact, I've discovered, as has Kai, who's expressed thanks for continuing access to the best book in the world.

From Cradle to Classroom

No sane parent would willingly keep a preschooler in a body cast for the first few years of life and then expect the child, freed from the limitations, to skip around the playground on the first day of school. Muscles would have atrophied. None of the crucial preliminary skills, such as standing and crawling, would have been learned. Yet some people neglect to provide brain stimulation and language-related play that, begun in the cradle, predict success in the classroom.

Read-aloud time with high-quality books should be a component of any child-care or preschool program. Asset 25, early literacy, in particular, highlights language-rich activities and print materials. Take an inventory of what's currently available in your home or preschool setting:

* What are the books' physical condition? Worn or untouched? Is there an ever-changing variety?
* Are age-appropriate books accessible to children for independent enjoyment? Do preschoolers treat these books respectfully?
* Is there an annual budget for buying new titles? (Literacy leaders recommend group settings have at least seven books per child, adding two new titles for each preschooler per year.) Are there community partnerships or foundation funding for additions?
* Are a number of titles related by topic? Do learning centers feature book-related play?

Perhaps you could offer information and support to a provider or preschool director. Informing parents and providers of basic needs, raising funds to add more books, and rotating books from the public library are crucial ways to serve.

Where Did You Get Your Moccasins?

• •

by Bernelda Wheeler, illustrated by Herman Bekkering. Winnipeg, Canada: Peguis, 1992.

CHILDREN IN AN URBAN SCHOOL are curious about a classmate's new pair of moccasins. He answers each of their questions about how his grandmother, or *kookum,* made them. On the left side of certain two-page spreads (and on one entire spread), the illustrator juxtaposes a traditional Native practice (such as preparing a deer hide) with a diverse group of children, growing in number, as the boy reveals the history of his prized possession. The story is rich in illustrated assets—the kids responding to novelty with interest and curiosity, a vital home-school connection, and active engagement in a learning experience.

Before You Read Together

On the cover, a young boy wearing jeans and a turtleneck also sports an everyday shoe on one foot and a traditional fur-trimmed moccasin on the other. A boy and a girl look with curiosity at the other moccasin in his hand. Is this type of shoe or the term for it new to the child? Repeat the word together. Can the child guess where the moccasin came from? whether the pair belongs to the boy?

After You Read Aloud

- It's good practice to praise children for asking questions: "What an interesting question!" "I'm glad you asked that." Give them the message that it's smart to ask about what we don't understand. If a child has more questions about the traditional practices mentioned in this story or basic understandings (What is leather?

What is hunting? What does beadwork look like?), search for answers together, using the library for other nonfiction books, the Internet, and artifacts in museums, if available.

- Children have different names for Grandmother: *Nana, Grandma, Mamaw, Granny, Abuelita,* and *Kookum* represent some. Find out what the preschooler calls his grandmother(s) and why.
- Talk together about the child's ethnicity. Are there traditional practices that date back to her ancestors? Do his family members have possessions that reflect their background? Talk about and handle them.

Made with Love

One of the reasons the main character's moccasins are noteworthy is that they are homemade. So clearly are they "made from scratch" that by the story's end, everybody sees the humor in his answer to the question about where the beads for the beadwork come from—the store.

What does the preschooler own that has not come from a store or that someone made by hand? Does she realize that because it is handmade, it's one of a kind? Have you talked about the steps that went into making the item? Does he know the maker? Raising awareness of the time and talent involved increases appreciation for a belonging. Calling attention to the special nature of a gift made with love offers a new spin on what's worth valuing.

Provide "guided discovery" or thoughtful exploration of a handmade gift, talking about its parts, its step-by-step creation, its uses. Stress how to enjoy it and care for it at the same time. You can praise a child's gentle handling and storage of a handcrafted treasure. You can affirm a child's own creations as one of a kind, too, reminding him that nothing else in all the world is quite like it, just as there is no person quite like him or her in all the world either.

Try having your child give a hand. Maybe he could help sand the wood for a handcrafted birdhouse. Perhaps she could hold up skeins of yarn to roll into balls prior to someone's knitting project. Maybe he could help in making a recipe from scratch. Perhaps a relative, a neighbor, or a friend would be willing to demonstrate the stages for crafting a handmade object. Or your child could produce a simpler version or take part in a small way.

Paper Moccasins

As you look at various types of shoes in a store window, catalog, or closet, ask your preschooler what kinds she can name—boots, slippers, clogs, high heels, sneakers, loafers. Ask how we would keep our feet warm or protect them from cuts, water, snow, or insect bites, if we had no factory-made shoes.

Thinking about this need increases our appreciation of moccasins and helps us understand what a terrific invention they were for the first people who lived on American soil. Let your little one know that at times people still wear moccasins. Look at photographs of moccasins on the Internet at www.themoccshop.com. Look at shoes worn around the world by reading together *Shoes, Shoes, Shoes* by Ann Morris.

Encourage the preschooler to make some paper moccasins. To create painted moccasin cutouts, you'll need:

- ☐ Brown paper bag (a grocery or lunch bag will do)
- ☐ Cotton swabs
- ☐ Small jars of paint in bright colors as well as brown or black
- ☐ Paintbrush
- ☐ Pencil
- ☐ Construction or craft paper
- ☐ Scissors

1. From the paper bag, cut out a rectangle larger than the area needed for both of the child's feet.
2. Invite the child to rumple, squeeze, and twist the rectangle until the resulting texture is pliable and soft—closer to deerskin.
3. Ask the child to place each foot on the rectangle. Trace around each footprint, commenting that each person has a right and a left foot. Print *left* and *right* on the undersides.
4. With an illustration as a guide, draw a curved line to show the opening of each moccasin.
5. You may wish to use a different cotton swab for each color. On a corner of the brown paper, show how to dip enough paint to make dots. Let the child experiment with a few dots on the paper beyond the footprints.
6. Invite the child to make dots like beadwork on each moccasin, if desired. An older preschooler may wish to make a design or pattern, but it's the process, not the final product, that matters.

7. With short brushstrokes in black or brown, the child may wish to paint "fur" along the "openings" into which feet slip. Let the artwork dry.

8. Cut out each moccasin and, if desired, mount the pair on construction or craft paper.

To make wearable moccasins of felt for the child, find directions in *Native Crafts* by Maxine Trottier. Depending on the child's age and motivation, you can also do a simpler version of the activity, simply cutting around outlines of the feet and decorating the "feet" as the child wishes.

The First People

It's not too early to introduce children to traditional practices and historical events, as long as we offer information that's developmentally appropriate and true. We must take care to avoid books that simply reinforce stereotypes.

This particular book not only acknowledges a traditional craft from long ago—a time when this boy's ancestors were the first people to live in North America—but also it features a Native (aboriginal) child who lives in a contemporary world. In *Through Indian Eyes: The Native Experience in Books for Children,* edited by Beverly Slapin and Doris Seale, Seale points out that "while some white illustrators are careful to produce multiethnic pictures, they never include a Native American child." Such "missing persons" in books as well as biased portrayals damage young children's sense of self-worth. Moreover, children who lack positive exposure to lots of ways of being may come to devalue people who seem different from themselves.

Books are a wonderful resource for enlarging a young child's world and encouraging acceptance of differences and commonalities among people. Hands-on experiences also go a long way toward making information meaningful for preschoolers, in particular. Enjoying a bowl of popcorn, for example, you might point out that Native Americans were the first people to grow corn. Using a library CD or tape of authentic music of a tribal nation and moving to it makes another's tradition come alive. If your child is not already a part of this culture and aware of the traditions, attending a public powwow provides a firsthand experience of traditional dress and dances, and at the same time reinforces that Native Americans dress, act, and live like other people today.

Toot & Puddle: Puddle's ABC

by Holly Hobbie. Boston: Little, Brown, 2000.

THIS PERFECT PRESCHOOL ALPHABET BOOK is dedicated "for readers-to-be." Between the covers children encounter, among other surprises, a crocodile crunching carrots and zooming zucchini. Puddle, a popular pig who stars in a series of books with his best buddy Toot, has painted all the letters! This simple story, about a turtle learning to print his name as he learns the alphabet, manages to highlight 26 alliterative phrases. The words in a set each begin with a featured letter/sound in the alphabet. This book is an engaging introduction to combining certain letters to build a word or name and it shows ingenious examples of how recombining letters (e.g., from OTTO to TOOT) magically creates a new word. Laughter complements learning, as it perfectly promotes language-rich activities.

Before You Read Together

Some children will recognize Puddle immediately because of previous encounters with him and Toot. Not only does the lovable pair appear in other books by Holly Hobbie, but they've inspired a line of toys. In any case, the preschooler will probably guess from the cover that the book features illustrated alphabet letters not by a human grown-up, but by a comical pig in paint-spattered overalls.

After You Read Aloud

- Create a phrase that includes the child's first name and two other words that begin with the same letter (e.g., "Sophie Spitting Seeds" or "Jumping Jitterbug Justin"). These creations need not make sense; the point is to recognize and isolate each word's beginning sound. Perhaps your child will want to create phrases related to every family member or a friend's name.

- See which letters your child can identify. Compare these to letters of different font styles found in other books.

making friends with the Alphabet

The child familiar with 26 letters prior to kindergarten is more apt to crack the code that leads to success in reading and in school. Singing the familiar jingle that features the alphabet letters to the tune of "Twinkle, Twinkle, Little Star" is a time-honored way to introduce the basics.

However, it doesn't go far in giving a child meaningful associations with individual letters. Nor does it relay the message that a certain sound corresponds to a certain symbol (e.g., "buh" with B), or that these letters combine to make words in a meaningful context. Exposing a child to alphabet books and interactive learning tools, or manipulatives, is more enjoyable and effective.

* An inexpensive, colorful set of plastic, magnetic alphabet letters, found in most toy and discount stores, merits a place on a refrigerator, cookie sheet, or other magnetic surface where you can put together simple words, such as *HI, STOP,* and *I LOVE YOU,* in addition to the child's name and any other words he would like to see. Allow her to play with the letters at any time and to create pretend words.

* On a chalkboard or sidewalk, print a particular letter and invite the preschooler to dip a paintbrush in water and "erase" the letter. Older preschoolers and kindergartners may wish to write the letter itself before they "erase" it.

* Zero in on a letter of the week, demonstrating its sound and taking a tour of the space you share to find objects that begin with that sound and letter. Label each object for a week, if you wish.

* Or assemble a group of everyday objects that begin with the same letter (and sound) and place them in a lidded box or basket. A younger child can identify and say the names of such objects; an older child can add contributions to the mix and play a memory game, recalling the container's contents. For example, if the featured letter is B, the contents might include a ball, a brush, a barrette, a bottle of bubbles, a baby's bottle, a book, and a blue bandana.

* Incorporate materials such as an alphabet puzzle, alphabet tub toys, and alphabet blocks into a child's collection of playthings. Call attention to letters spied out in the world.

An Edible Alphabet

You can find cookie cutters with the shapes of the 26 alphabet letters in some cookware stores or certain educational catalogs. (See "Resources" on page 224 for information on a source of inexpensive cookie cutters.) Press out the alphabet letters at random; use X's and O's to represent kisses and hugs; or select the letters of the child's name or short words such as *wow, yes, hi, go,* and *eat.* Bake and ice the cookies with frosting to which you've added food coloring, if you wish. (We perched cookie cutter letters on one of our kitchen walls, each resting on a little nail, when my kids were preschoolers; they used them for play dough creations, too.) Here are recipes for cookies and icing:

LINDA'S ROLLOUT COOKIES

1/2 cup butter, softened

8 ounces cream cheese, softened

2 cups sugar

1 egg

1 teaspoon vanilla extract

1/4 teaspoon almond extract

3 1/2 cups flour

1 teaspoon baking powder

1. Preheat oven to 325°F.
2. Cream butter and cream cheese. Add sugar. Mix until fluffy.
3. Add egg, vanilla, and almond extract.
4. In a separate bowl, mix flour and baking powder.
5. Add the egg mixture to the flour mix. Beat just until mixed. Chill.
6. Roll out a third of the dough at a time, first placing under floured waxed paper. Remove waxed paper and cut out letter shapes with cookie cutters.
7. Place on ungreased cookie sheets.
8. Bake for 18 minutes. Cool before icing.

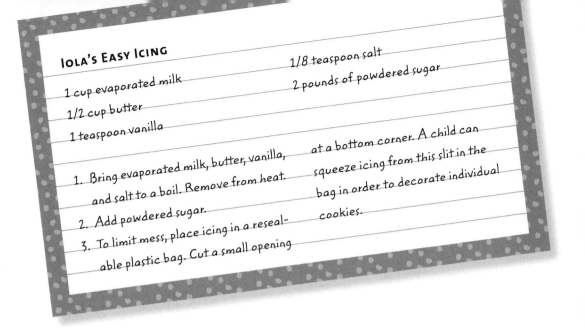

IOLA'S EASY ICING

1 cup evaporated milk

1/2 cup butter

1 teaspoon vanilla

1/8 teaspoon salt

2 pounds of powdered sugar

1. Bring evaporated milk, butter, vanilla, and salt to a boil. Remove from heat.

2. Add powdered sugar.

3. To limit mess, place icing in a resealable plastic bag. Cut a small opening at a bottom corner. A child can squeeze icing from this slit in the bag in order to decorate individual cookies.

Delight from A to Z

One of the most enjoyable ways to make introductions to the alphabet is to seek out and share captivating books in which each letter stars. As you meander through the pages, you can make a game of hunting for a specific letter or counting how many times it appears on the cover or on a page. A child can look for letters that appear in his own name. She can find illustrated items that begin with a certain sound or letter.

Point out lowercase and uppercase (capital) letters when they appear side by side. And let the preschooler pore over such books independently. Gradually, despite illustrators' stylized variants of letters, a child grasps the essence, the basic form of each. Repeat visits reinforce what a source of pleasure letter combinations can be, magically creating words and imagined worlds. The following books are letter-perfect—especially engaging for preschoolers and the kindergarten set:

Alfie's ABC by Shirley Hughes

Alphabet Under Construction by Denise Fleming

Chicka Chicka Boom Boom by Bill Martin Jr. and John Archambault

Flora McDonnell's ABC by Flora McDonnell

Mouse Letters: A Very First Alphabet Book by Jim Arnosky

Museum ABC edited by Judith Cressy of the Metropolitan Museum of Art

Toot & Puddle: Puddle's ABC by Holly Hobbie (featured here on page 119)

The Jamie and Angus Stories

by Anne Fine, illustrated by Penny Dale. Cambridge, MA: Candlewick Press, 2002.

BECAUSE THIS BOOK about preschooler Jamie and his beloved toy Highland bull, Angus, is presented in six chapters, it is an unusual format for the preschool set. However, preschoolers whose maturity level makes it possible to listen to longer stories will find the content right on target. Enjoy vignettes about Angus's ordeal in the washing machine, Uncle Edward's unusual bedtime rituals, a babysitter's wedding day, the day Daddy ditches the stroller, a stay in the hospital, and Jamie's daylong experiment to live like a grown-up. Older siblings also can enjoy this book that highlights one boy's ongoing commitment to learning.

Before You Read Together

On the back cover, a boy stares intently at a gift-wrapped package. On the front cover, he holds aloft the unwrapped toy animal. The title reveals that inside more than one story is waiting. Big kids call it a chapter book because one can read each story or chapter in different sittings. Even if the format is one commonly associated with older readers, the narrative of this book is clearly about and for a preschooler. You'll want to be sure to read the first chapter before any others to understand the history of Jamie and Angus coming together.

After You Read Aloud

- A few words in this British import will merit explanation as you encounter them, specifically "idling in the bloody stroller." You can easily translate this phrase to something like "relaxing in the darned stroller."

- If your child has a favorite doll, stuffed animal, cape, imaginary friend, or other loved object, recall its history. Who gave it? How long has it been around? What does he like best about it? What's a favorite adventure involving it? Where does it stay when it's away from her? Encourage the preschooler to invent a story about it.
- Name the feelings Jamie and others have in each story. Emphasize that all of our feelings are okay.

Buried Treasure

Each chapter in this book happens to involve a grown-up who models behavior that makes an event memorable in young Jamie's life. What creative or compassionate or caring thing could you do to add a memorable "chapter" to your child's year? Once, we hosted a birthday party for preschoolers-turned-pirates (bloody pirates, matey!). But you don't need a birthday to make this event special. In the spirit of fun, produce the items below, and make a memory to treasure.

- ☐ Pirate garb for two: eye patches, striped shirt, colorful scarf to wear as a head wrap, gaudy jewelry, foil-covered squares for shoe buckles, ragged pants or long skirt(s), etc.
- ☐ Pirate gear: small shovels, handmade treasure map (described below), storybook, pirate flag, plush parrot
- ☐ Large sack
- ☐ Treasure: gold foil–covered chocolate coins, play money, old necklaces, other flea market baubles, and/or a coupon for a surprise treat (a movie, an outing), and a container (small wooden chest, cardboard gift box, or tin container) in which to keep it all

1. In advance, gather items. Put costumes and your map in the sack.
2. Out of sight of the child, in a place where the treasure is safe, dig a shallow hole.
3. Into the hole, place the container filled with the treasure.
4. Prepare a treasure map. Draw simple symbols for familiar neighborhood or backyard sites (a mailbox, a sandbox, a bird feeder, a back porch) and thoroughly wrinkle up the paper, tearing edges and applying a stain of tea or coffee to make it look old and weathered.

5. Cut or tear the paper to make separate smaller sections, one for each picture of a site or drawn symbol. Hide each in the order you wish for the treasure hunt, with the *last* picture clue sending the little pirate to the site of the buried treasure.

6. When the child least expects it, appear with an eye patch and the sack containing the clothes and map. At this point, you may wish to read aloud a book like *Maisy's Pirate Treasure Hunt* by Lucy Cousins.

7. "Discover" the treasure map portion and don the pirate garb.

8. Follow the map to the treasure, digging for the loot together.

"New and Improved" Childhood

Your answers to three questions may alter how you connect with kids daily:

1. When the children in my life are grown, what will they remember most about me?

2. Years from now, what will I feel about how I shaped our time together?

3. Looking back at my own childhood, what do I wish had been different, and what did I miss?

The young character Jamie is blessed with parents who are confident and kind, firm but loving. Can such stories be meaningful for children who live in different and more dismal circumstances than his? Author Anne Fine, for one, says they can. Accepting the Boston Globe-Horn Book Award for best fiction, she noted that through books, "even the youngest child perceives that there are other ways of living and loving, that, in short, there will always be choices." Such asset-rich books shed a light as well on choices possible for parents and others who care about pre-schoolers. Here's Fine again, on the power of eye-opening literature:

> *Perhaps you drew the short straw with your own family, surroundings, and supports. But . . . learning about a family like Jamie's can offer a shaft of light that shows the way out of a dark place. We know from our experience, and that of others, how very often even the unspoken "I wish things were like that for me" has been translated by sheer human grit and determination over years, into "but I have made things very different for my own children."*

Ginny, a friend, endured one dispiriting experience after another in childhood, but she has engaged in such mindful parenting herself. No one—parent or teacher—need be a prisoner of the past. The commitment to learning that adults hope children possess is more likely if their caregivers are committed to learning as well. To do something new and improved:

* Release yourself from feeling you're bound to repeat mistakes adults made who cared for you. They did what they could. Your best effort, your responses, can be different.

* Visualize or list a few ways you'd like to improve on your own childhood.

* Let go of any mistakes you've made with your child or young charges. In your mind's eye, see your improved action or reaction. Mentally rehearse it and follow through at the next opportunity.

* List strengths you already possess. Look for guidance. For example, to gauge what a child is able to handle and to state reasonable expectations, visit the Talaris Research Institute Web site (www. talaris.org), which features developmental benchmarks from birth to age 5.

Live and Learn

The experience chart is a useful aid. Typically, a pre-K teacher asks children to volunteer what they know about an object or area of interest both before and after activities or stories related to that subject. The grown-up prints the children's contributions on a large piece of chart paper for all to see. Preschoolers observe their spoken words transformed into print. The chart calls attention to literacy's power, for, magically, all who know how to read can repeat, at any time, the exact words the preschoolers have provided. It's also a tool to assess their learning.

The asset framework is a potent reminder, however, of many more kinds of learning that come into play in the preschool years. Author Anne Fine alludes to this ongoing information gathering: "Jamie is learning, learning, learning—right through from the trivia of finding out whether or not he likes the taste of olives to how to be . . . courteous and (up to a point) selfless at weddings." Invite a young learner to talk about such learning and what, at the moment, matters: "Did you try something new today? What do you want most to learn how to do? What are you happy you know how to do already? What are you getting better and better at? Did you hear about something new today that you didn't know before?"

Resist the temptation to pigeonhole children, judging what each is capable of and prescribing every minute of their being and doing. Each deserves precious time for exploration that, yes, includes the ABCs but encompasses so much more. Children's living is their learning.

Author William Martin's words, in *The Parent's Tao Te Ching: Ancient Advice for Modern Parents—A New Interpretation,* are applicable to any adult who spends time with children:

INFINITE POSSIBILITIES

You do not know the true origin of your children.
You call them yours
but they belong to a greater Mystery.
You do not know the name of this Mystery,
but it is the true Mother and Father of your children.

At birth your children are filled with possibilities.
It is not your job to limit these possibilities.
Do not say, "This and that are possible for you.
These other things are not."
They will discover on their own what is and is not possible.
It is your job to help them stay open to the marvelous mysteries of life.

Commitment-to-Learning Bonus Best Bets

- **Alfie's ABC** by Shirley Hughes. New York: Lothrop, Lee & Shepard Books, 1998.

- **At School: A Lift-the-Flap Learning Book** by Francisco Pittau and Bernadette Gervais. Éditions du Seuil. San Francisco: Chronicle Books, 2003.

- **Curious Kids Go to Preschool: Another Big Book of Words** by Heloise Antoine, illustrated by Ingrid Godon. Atlanta, GA: Peachtree, 1996.

- **First Day** by Dandi Daley Mackall. San Diego: Harcourt, 2003.

- **Sammy and the Dinosaurs** by Ian Whybrow, illustrated by Adrian Reynolds. New York: Orchard Books, 1999. See also, by the same author, **Harry and the Bucketful of Dinosaurs**.

- **Talking Like the Rain** selected by X. J. and Dorothy Kennedy. Boston: Little, Brown, 1992.

- **Usborne First 100 Words in Spanish** by Heather Amery, illustrated by Stephen Cartwright, with translation and pronunciation guide by Jane Straker. London: Usborne, 2002 (U.S. edition).

Positive Values

In Hardwired to Connect: The New Scientific Case for Authoritative Communities, *published by The Commission on Children at Risk, we learn something most of us have suspected—that all humans are hardwired to connect with other people. Given the chance, given human models, the young come to understand what it means to be a good person, to live a good, healthy life. Early on, if they are lucky, if somebody is building assets in everyday interactions, young children learn about equality and social justice. With encouragement, through trial and error, they learn, too, what caring, honesty, and responsibility look like. Their families model living a healthy lifestyle. They begin to identify integrity through meaningful exchanges in life and through the pages of their books.*

• •

ESSENTIAL ELEMENTS TO LOOK FOR in books we choose and use are those that increase children's appreciation of beauty and their enthusiasm for life, those that promote a healthy, happy lifestyle. Without being dreary or preachy, books can socialize young children in powerful ways. Stories inspire their best impulses. They reflect their best instincts. Books offer a comfortable way to preview situations that call for caring or honesty or restraint—any number of positive values.

Characters embody a responsible and responsive way of being in the world. There's Jamela, who makes a mistake that pains her mother, just like other preschoolers who make mistakes and learn from them, too. Or Ping, honest about failure when even his best efforts lead to disappointing results. And there's Alfie, who shows empathy for his younger sister, for the bashful guest at a birthday party, for the sitter—already doing what he can, in each instance, to offer help and comfort to others in distress.

Stella, Queen of the Snow

. . . .

by Marie-Louise Gay. Toronto: Groundwood/Douglas & McIntyre, 2000.

CANADIAN AUTHOR AND ILLUSTRATOR Marie-Louise Gay charms children and grown-ups alike in her series about irrepressible Stella and her little brother Sam. In this story, Sam pelts his big sister with questions about their wintry world. She, in turn, relishes her role as an authority on everything. The self-confident big sister, who is not much older than her younger sibling, and Sam, who is alternately eager for, and wary of, his sister's impulses, offer a vivid reminder of what developmental differences exist even in children fairly close in age—and what acceptance is possible between peers or siblings, a focus of this category of Developmental Assets.

Before You Read Together

On the cover, Stella stands with outstretched arms and a smile that welcomes readers into her world. She's open to the possibilities created by a snowy day *and* she's poised to offer you a bear hug. Her brother, barely beyond toddler age, is pictured on the back. He appears less exuberant but willing to venture out with his sister. Welcome to a youngster's first experience with snow that even children in tropical climes can revel in.

After You Read Aloud

- Depending on the age of the child and any prior experiences with snow, she may be as gullible as Sam or as savvy as Stella about the white stuff. Enjoy talking together about some of Stella's claims (e.g., birds wear snow boots). Discuss what is fact and what is Stella's brand of make-believe or fiction. Let the child lead as you distinguish between the two.

- Point out and reinforce concepts such as *under, over, behind, below, inside, outside,* and *above*—still new to the child using these terms to establish location of objects in the world.

Frosted Flakes

Just as there are no two people exactly alike, no two snowflakes are the same either.

I know preschool teachers who supply their charges with simple sheets of black construction paper in order to reveal this natural wonder. On days short on wind and long on snow crystals in the air, you and the child can follow suit, letting the flakes alight on the paper for closer inspection.

Or you can create in advance a simple, reusable snowflake landing pad that's easier to hold in mitten-covered hands. You'll need:

- ❑ A small piece of foam board (from an art or office supply store)
- ❑ A piece of black felt of the dimensions of the foam board
- ❑ Glue
- ❑ A magnifying glass

Glue the felt to the board. When flurries are forecast, stick the board in the freezer—at least long enough for the board to get cold and keep captured flakes intact longer. When the snow starts falling, bundle up the kids and go fishing for flakes, catching them on the lightweight board. Study them outside under the magnifying glass. Celebrate each flake's uniqueness.

Here's an option for warmer climates: Ahead of time cut white gift wrap tissue into 4- or 6-inch squares. Fold each square in half. Fold it in half again. Draw a curved line from one open corner to the other and cut. Demonstrate and assist cutting triangles and other shapes of various sizes from all three edges into the paper. Let preschoolers use safety scissors. Carefully unfold tissue and glue each snowflake to a window or to dark blue or black paper. Let it snow!

Supportive Siblings

The character Sam seems very naive and vulnerable, but Stella never takes advantage of him. She does not bait or tease her little brother, nor abandon him or consciously mislead him. She does her thing and is accepting when he joins in, as when the pair make snow angels and listen for their singing. Does the story read like a tall tale? Or do such relations exist in your household?

Experts suggest that the closer in age siblings are to one another, the more often problems can arise. However, adults can take steps to minimize problems, and should. Just because such friction is normal— that is, widespread—doesn't mean it's healthy, researchers say. Certain responses by adults to sisters' and brothers' interactions can shape lifelong negative attitudes about the self and one's family.

For starters, adults and children alike can find guidance and inspiration in books. The best-selling classic *Siblings without Rivalry* by Adele Faber and Elaine Mazlish is packed with effective methods and important insights for adults willing to promote peaceful and positive relationships between sibs.

And young children benefit from seeing such relationships play out in the pages of their books. Worthy of mention are Shirley Hughes's books about preschooler Alfie and his little sister, such as *Rhymes for Annie Rose* and *The Big Alfie and Annie Rose Storybook*. Additional books about siblings include *Big Brother, Little Brother* by Penny Dale, *Big Brother Dustin* by Dan Young with Carol Carter, *I Can't Talk Yet but When I Do . . .* by Julie Markes, and *Tell Me Something Happy Before I Go to Sleep* by Joyce Dunbar.

Give Them Wings

Add some pizzazz to outdoor snow angels simply by filling a spray bottle with water. Add food coloring in a desired color. Have the preschooler spray an area of the snow angel with the color. Refill the bottle with water and another chosen color. Let the child spray away again. Repeat while the child is engaged with the process. Add button eyes and a halo of glitter, if you wish.

Here's an indoor alternative: Have the child lie with legs outstretched and arms near sides on a large piece of butcher paper, an old white sheet, or a piece of solid colored fabric. (If you use fabric, first spray or saturate it with fabric stiffener and let it dry.) First, outline the child's outer legs, but instead of outlining the inner legs, draw a line between the two heels (for the angel's gown or robe hem).

Then, outline the actual arms and the rest of the body. Afterward, ask the child to stretch out both arms at shoulder height. Draw a line along the top of each arm and place a dot at the location of each middle finger. Lower both arms a few inches. Draw another dot near each middle fingernail. Lower again, adding dots. Use the dots to draw the outline of wings. With glitter or sequins sprinkled over lines of glue, embellish the wings. Color in details with marker.

Jamela's Dress

• •

by Niki Daly. New York: Farrar, Straus and Giroux, 1999.

JAMELA OFFERS TO KEEP AN EYE on some beautiful new fabric for her mother as it dries on the line. On a whim, she parades around town in the material. Mama and other grown-ups are upset when the fabric—intended for a special dress—is returned soiled and torn. This tale portrays a South African preschooler short on impulse control who gets in hot water until a young photographer saves the day. The supportive community is quick to reinforce positive values and forgive a lapse in good judgment by "Kwela Jamela, African Queen."

Before You Read Together

The girl on the cover, likely to be Jamela, is playing dress-up with a grown-up's high heels and a long swath of brightly patterned fabric. A curious rooster and playful dog look on, so she appears to be outdoors. The endpapers repeat the fabric pattern and the title page reveals an appreciative crowd cheering on Miss Make-Believe. The child you're reading with is likely to predict that the fabric is Jamela's, since the title notes that a dress is hers. But as the story unfolds, it becomes clear that Jamela has overstepped her bounds.

After You Read Aloud

- Let the child roll the words of the chant around on the tongue and chime in whenever any of the characters say, " Kwela Jamela, African Queen." Discover the African meanings of the word *kwela*, paraphrasing the information in the author's note at the back. Can the child you're sharing the book with think of one or more words or sounds that rhyme with his own name?

- Visit a fabric store and touch different fabrics. Look at fabric patterns, noticing how designs repeat. If a field trip isn't possible, collect small pieces of various material to examine. Talk about which fabric the child likes best.
- Provide a large piece of material, ideally that the child has chosen, and invite her to act out the story with you or with playmates or siblings who have heard the tale as well. Parade like Jamela, to drumbeats or a CD or tape of African music.

Camera Ready

The first photos my son took when he was almost 5 were nothing to crow about: I remember telephone wires, a blurry fishbowl, the "headless" torso of a next-door neighbor. I decided that he was just not ready to use a camera. The truth of the matter was that *I* was not ready for him to use one. For me, the grown-up, picture taking was all about the final product.

I feel differently now. I might have studied what had sparked his interest, using his subject matter as a springboard for discussion about why he'd taken the pictures he did. I might have recognized how empowering it is for a young prereader to visually record his world. I recall that he wasn't disappointed with how the photos turned out. He had enjoyed the experience as well as the magical results. I was the only one bent on building competency.

A disposable camera can be a source of all kinds of learning that have little to do with producing a prize-winning picture like that of the photographer in the story. Practice makes perfect, of course. It's probable that with each successive roll of film, my preschooler's pictures would have improved. The point, however, is that the experience itself is worth prizing.

An adult reading aloud the camera directions models for the preschooler an important function of the printed word. Studying the camera parts through guided discovery satisfies the preschooler's curiosity and, with a few clicks, offers her a chance for a trial run. Invite your child to take spontaneous pictures or determine a focus for his attention. Having a particular subject or theme in mind fosters thinking skills. Following are photographic possibilities:

* A special occasion such as a wedding, photographed from the child's point of view.
* The faces (or knees!) of favorite people, or still lifes of favorite belongings.
* Several objects all of one color or an example of each color (see books by Tana Hoban).
* A familiar object photographed from different angles (above, below, far away, up close).
* Patterns in nature and in objects, with repeating designs, as in Jamela's mother's fabric.

No camera within reach? Invite a child to make a circle with the thumb and index finger and look through the hole (the make-believe lens) to find a sight to "capture," such as a person, object, or scene he wants to remember always.

Natural Consequences

Jamela is just beginning to be aware that her actions affect others. She is not intentionally willful or naughty. Hers are the first missteps on a long journey of learning the meaning and impact of her actions. It's the same journey every preschooler has begun.

Jamela's distress is a natural consequence of her forgetfulness. Her mother does not hide her sadness over the ruined fabric, but neither does she punish nor lash out at her child. Jamela already feels embarrassed and sad that she has brought on her mother's misery. This parent knows her child has learned a lesson without having to be humiliated or spanked. Resorting to lecturing ("Didn't you promise to look after the fabric?") or shaming ("What a bad girl you are!") only serves to make Jamela and other children of her age feel guilty or frightened.

When a preschooler misbehaves, ask yourself if your expectations are age-appropriate. Always seek to determine the cause of the misbehavior before you act:

* Did a child not fully understand a rule or boundary? This calls for a clearer explanation or a loving reminder.
* Does the child simply need attention? If this is the cause, give that attention or promise it shortly and deliver on your pledge. Most children who generally feel noticed or included and routinely have their basic needs met do not misbehave very often.

✱ Was the child testing limits or lacking in self-control? In either case, be firm about boundaries. Say, for example, "It's a mistake to go into the cookie jar without permission," and then figure out with the child a natural consequence—perhaps fewer cookies after supper.

In any case, separate the child from the behavior. Recognize the difference between "I don't like it when you . . ." and "I don't like you." Jamela's mother practices forgiveness and models its power for her child. Despite her disappointment, this wise parent recognizes that discipline is about teaching, not about punishment. Responses that humiliate or hurt children accomplish nothing. Impulse control and self-discipline come after repeated reminders, patient guidance, and consistent nurturing.

Read All about It

Discovering her picture in the newspaper is a bittersweet experience for Jamela because the parading that resulted in a prize-winning photo also led to Mama's ruined material. For others, Jamela's picture provides an opportunity for a positive story on the front page! See if you can select, at home or at the library, a newspaper with happy news in the headlines—a team championship or a medical breakthrough. At very least, choose an edition that does not contain horrific front-page pictures. Then take a tour of the paper with the preschooler.

✱ Point out the largest print, saying it's reserved for the most important headlines and stories.

✱ Explain the sections of the paper devoted to national and local news, sports, business and finance, and the arts.

✱ See if you can find an ad or picture related to a film you are planning to see or have enjoyed.

✱ Look at the comics page and read a simple strip or two.

✱ Look for familiar corporate logos in the ads and explain that stores and companies pay money to the newspaper to use its pages to attract customers.

✱ Tell about photographers and reporters—real people whose job it is to take the pictures (like Archie) and to write the news stories.

* Let the child ask questions about items of interest. Using a discarded newspaper, she may want to cut out the letters in ads and headlines that she recognizes, that are in her name, or that spell out words.
* Isolate a page such as the want ads as a background for a pattern. Take two halves of a potato or a cucumber and cut designs into them. Or, cut two sponges into different shapes. Now let the child dip one into a saucer of paint, then dip the other into a different color. Encourage the child to make a pattern (e.g., two red triangles, one yellow oval, two red triangles, one yellow oval), altering the chosen pattern on different areas of the sheet.
* Occasionally share news stories that you think the preschooler would find interesting.

The Tomten

. . . .

by Astrid Lindgren. New York: Puffin, 1997.

CALLED "A PICTURE BOOK OF RARE DISTINCTION" by the *Chicago Tribune* and "a gentle story with eye-filling scenes" by *Publishers Weekly, The Tomten,* written by the 1958 winner of the Hans Christian Andersen Award and reissued many times, is a favorite of generations of young children. The gnomelike tomten is the guardian of a humble home-stead, following through on simple tasks that help or benefit others over hundreds of winters. At night, he goes about his secret rounds, visiting the animals and checking on the sleeping children, in a gentle, loving manner. The refrain—"winters come and winters go, summers come and summers go"—honors the predictability of the seasons and the comforting presence of those who love us.

Before You Read Together

On this wintry night, no one seems to be awake or about except for an elf-like person with a full white beard and a red stocking cap. Ask the child: "Who is this creature on the cover? Where is he going?"

After You Read Aloud

- On rereadings, invite the child to chime in on "winters come and winters go," providing as much of the refrain as he can remember. Relish the quiet introduction, already knowing what's to come—a visit from the tomten.
- No people have seen the tomten. Perhaps he is just make-believe. Only the animals know for sure. Sometimes children look for his footprints in the snow. Find out if there are other figures in the child's life that add magic to her days? Can you make room for the possibility of such an invisible friend? If possible, visit a store that sells Scandinavian crafts to see tomtenlike figurines.

- The tomten gives milk to the hungry cat. Otherwise, he simply "stands watch." Talk about ways we show, without words, that we care about someone.

Feed the Birds

The preschooler can check on the status of seed in any store-bought bird feeders in your yard or on the grounds of your organization. She can perform an important service—feeding the least among us. We mounted our favorite feeder (with suction cups) on glass. At the kitchen window, birds breakfasted when we did. At a bedroom window, wildlife became a source of ongoing interest. In the absence of such feeders or in addition to them, together make your own versions.

FRUIT OR PINECONE FEEDERS

- ☐ Large apple or orange (and optional extra apple)
- ☐ Large pinecones from outside or plant/craft stores
- ☐ Sharp knife (for an adult's use)
- ☐ Ribbon or string cut in 8-inch to 12-inch lengths
- ☐ Scissors
- ☐ Plastic knife and spoon
- ☐ Peanut butter
- ☐ Birdseed
- ☐ Optional: sunflower/thistle seeds, cranberries, chunks of fruit, cereal, raisins, coconut

As the child watches, cut the fruit into 1-inch to 2-inch slices. Leave the apple's skin on to attract the birds. Cut or poke a small hole into each slice. After the child threads a string through each hole, tie the ends into a knot. Let the child spread peanut butter on one side of each slice and, by hand or spoon, sprinkle the birdseed onto the peanut butter base. Suspend from branches or shrubs within view.

In a similar fashion, tie a loop of string to a pinecone. Then, using a plastic knife or spoon, let the child spread peanut butter onto portions of the pinecone. Sprinkle with birdseed, sunflower or thistle seed, or bits of fruit.

Make an extra apple into a "walking salad" for the child to eat as you explore the possibilities for feeding stations or as you enjoy bird-watching outdoors together. Here's how to do it: Core an apple, and fill the opening with peanut butter. Add raisins and, if the child wishes, garnish it with coconut. Keep a simple bird guidebook on hand to identify visitors to your homemade feeders.

Feed the Tomten

Each winter, when my children were young, we mixed, baked, and placed on our back doorstep a simple rice porridge. We made the effort, just in case a tomten, not unlike the one in Astrid Lindgren's classic, had adopted our neighborhood. Though ours was admittedly low on livestock, there was always the chance that a tomten lovingly watched over us!

This ritual of giving prompted almost as much suspense and excitement as receiving gifts at Christmas. These preschoolers were always eager to discover whether a tomten had found the gift on our porch step during the night. (Oddly enough, the food invariably disappeared, though I'm not sure if the diner was a tomten, a tabby, or a fat raccoon.) Use your own recipe for rice pudding or bake this very simple version, making sure you enjoy some of it yourselves!

GUDRUN'S RICE PUDDING

4 cups of milk

1 stick of cinnamon

1/2 cup of rice (converted, not instant)

1–2 teaspoons vanilla

1/2 teaspoon salt

1/2 cup sugar

1. Preheat oven to 325° F.
2. Mix together ingredients and place in a baking dish.
3. The adult should stir the mixture periodically until a golden brown crust begins to form. Bake until all the milk is absorbed and the crust is browned, between 3 and 4 hours.

Feed the World

Perhaps your child is already involved in a program or practice that feeds the hungry. If a field trip is possible, volunteer at a soup kitchen together. Like the family in Hilary Horder Hippely's *A Song for Lena,* you and the child may have fed a hungry stranger who appeared in your life. Perhaps the child has watched you make or deliver a loving offering of food to a grieving neighbor or sick friend. The child's congregation may host the homeless at meals where congregants serve and/or dine with those in need of food and companionship.

If you're looking for a concrete way to model concern for the hungry in this world, contributing to any of a number of nonprofit projects is one option. For example, a heifer spells hope for children who need milk. Goats, sheep, llamas, pigs, geese, ducks, and bees all provide forms of nutrition and livelihood for families in the world who want to survive and become self-sufficient. Heifer International is an organization that connects these animals with families, thanks to the donations of others. The charity is an especially appropriate choice for involving preschoolers because they are able to form a concrete image of what their donation provides, ranging from relatively inexpensive chicks to water buffalo.

The organization's colorful catalog features real families and the animals that have brought them food and income. The organization provides a foldout card (among other options) that explains how the gift will make a life-changing difference to a family in need. With ringing endorsements from people such as former president Jimmy Carter, Oprah Winfrey, and Walter Cronkite, this not-for-profit organization may provide a meaningful way to commemorate a birthday, to remember less fortunate families on a religious holy day, or to celebrate an annual holiday such as Valentine's Day. For a catalog or additional information, contact Heifer International, www.heifer.org, 800-698-2511.

All About Alfie

. . . .

by Shirley Hughes. New York: Lothrop, Lee & Shepard Books/Morrow Junior Books, 1997.

ORIGINALLY PUBLISHED AS SEPARATE BOOKS *(Alfie Gets in First, Alfie's Feet, Alfie Gives a Hand,* and *An Evening at Alfie's),* this classic collection of stories features preschooler Alfie, his little sister Annie Rose, and his parents dealing with everyday challenges in their friendly, urban neighborhood. Young listeners will recognize themselves in Alfie, as he goes with his favorite blanket to his first birthday party. They'll sympathize when he accidentally locks his mother and sister out of the house and finds he can't quite reach the doorknob to let them in. They'll relate when Alfie gets a pair of new boots for splashing in puddles and puts each one on the wrong foot. And they'll admire the part he plays upon discovering a big leak in the ceiling after his parents have left him and his sister with Maureen, their babysitter.

Hughes's colorful illustrations of a down-to-earth family and caring neighbors are chock-full of realistic details, including the clutter that seems a part of any household with young children. The text highlights a range of positive values, including caring, concern for people, integrity, and responsibility. Preschoolers who make friends with Alfie will welcome other stories in which he stars, including a somewhat older Alfie in *Annie Rose Is My Little Sister.*

Before You Read Together

Heeeeere's Alfie! Your preschooler is likely to guess that the boy cavorting on the cover is Alfie. However, be sure to verify that the five illustrated boys are not quintuplets, but one person shown doing different things. Veteran readers take for granted that the boy or boat in one frame is the same in another. Children just learning about the conventions of print may need to know, however, that the same object or character appears again and again. You may wish to preread the four stories and dive into one that's especially pertinent to the preschooler's experience. In any case, respect a child's attention span, savoring one or two stories per session.

After You Read Aloud

- Discover what details prompt comments and questions from the child and focus on those after each reading.

Peacekeepers

All About Alfie depicts a child showing empathy, understanding, and awareness of others' feelings, significant elements of asset 26, caring. When the baby cries inconsolably, we read that Alfie "put his hand through the bars of her crib and patted her very gently as he had seen Mom do sometimes." He provides a reassuring presence to another guest at a birthday party, even though, unsure himself, he has felt the need to bring his blanket along to the festivities. He embodies the quality of caring that makes it possible for even young children to "make comforting and accepting gestures to peers and others in distress" and "to show concern for people who are at a disadvantage." How has this preschooler managed to integrate such positive values so early?

We need not look far. The stories show that he has adults in his life building these very assets, not only by their own example but also by their treatment of Alfie. The people in his world actively and consciously keep the peace, whether joining in a neighborhood rescue effort to help his mother reach Alfie, locked in the house, or, once calm prevails, celebrating together over "a spot of tea." When Alfie makes a mistake, his parents are understanding and forgiving so that Alfie's dignity remains intact. Children like Alfie are always watching. He absorbs the values the grown-ups around him demonstrate and practices doing likewise when opportunities arise. Keep in mind the caring examples of Alfie's significant others for models of real-world actions:

- ✱ Refuse to lock any child into a role, whether it be "little devil" or "perfect angel."
- ✱ Give each sibling or member of a group focused individual attention from time to time.
- ✱ Practice random acts of kindness to loved ones and strangers.

* Affirm anyone, including the child, who performs a caring act on behalf of another.
* Preserve the peace, sibling to sibling. (If competition or conflict is the norm, find wise counsel in a classic like Faber and Mazlish's *Siblings Without Rivalry*.)

Lifesavors

Alfie's needs are simple—a pair of new boots and a trek to the park with Dad, a blanket for courage at his first birthday party away from home, a cookie and a cuddle with his sister once the ceiling leak is fixed and her diaper's dry. Children value the simplest of love offerings.

An old list of "lifesavors" for our then 3-year-old daughter, Liv, included a giant box of crayons, a roll of tape, a real lunch box, cookie cutters, a letter in the mailbox, straws, a present "just because," a turn at the sink "washing" dishes, an open lap, and a packet of seeds.

Surely somewhere in Alfie's house, there is another lifesavor—a large, plastic box with a lid or a deep drawer, holding all manner of art supplies. If Annie Rose and Alfie want to sponge-paint over dinosaur or duck stencils, if they decide to make an early valentine for Grandma, or if Mom decides that they can fingerpaint with instant pudding, accompanied by her favorite tunes, the very things they need will be at their fingertips. Here's what you might include in an art box or corner:

□ Child-safe scissors
□ Glitter
□ Pencils, sharpener
□ Pens
□ Clear contact paper
□ Glue, glue sticks
□ Resealable plastic bags
□ Colored pencils, markers, chalk
□ Hole punch
□ Sponges
□ Stencils
□ Construction paper
□ Liquid starch
□ Stapler

□ Paper clips
□ Crayons
□ Newsprint
□ Paper
□ Stickers
□ Lengths of ribbon, yarn, and string
□ Fabric paint
□ Old magazines
□ Cards
□ Straws
□ Food coloring
□ Paints
□ Paintbrushes
□ Tape

At our house, a painted pegboard by the back door got lots of use. Hooks held layer upon layer of both kids' artwork, certificates, and mementos—wonders to enjoy daily in passing.

Breathing In and Out

Exasperating or challenging moments we have with young children can make a good story when recounted in a book such as *All About Alfie* or relived through a humorous retelling. As we are living through them, however, the humor may be lost on us.

I am fingering a dog-eared copy of the book I turned to often when my own children were small, its pages now marked with rust-encrusted paper clips! *Whole Child, Whole Parent* by Polly Berrien Berends restored my sense of balance and purpose when the responsibility for raising children felt overwhelming. The title itself reminded me that my children were already whole and as likely to be my teachers as I was theirs. Inspired by the wisdom of many faith traditions, the author wryly concludes, "Parenthood is just the world's most intensive course in love." This statement rings true for anyone who spends time with a child. The effect on me was to remember to breathe and to take heart.

One can reserve a few minutes a day to teach a lifelong skill for finding inner peace. "Taking a breather" in the midst of a busy world gains new meaning when one associates this conscious practice with the 5,000-year-old tradition of yoga. Yoga teachers note that young children have an instinctive ability to focus their breath and to watch how their bodies respond. Why not breathe together? In a quiet space, invite your child to follow your lead.

1. To keep the spine straight, lie on your backs, with legs shoulder-width apart. Place one palm up on the floor and the other gently resting on your abdomen ("tummy").
2. Close your eyes and breathe in slowly through the nose. Feel an imaginary balloon fill up and make the tummy rise.
3. Slowly breathe out through the nose and feel the "balloon" empty as the tummy flattens under one's hand. Repeat several times. Welcome a renewed sense of peace and calm.

The Empty Pot

by Demi. New York: Henry Holt, 1990.

AN OLD EMPEROR IN CHINA creates a clever plan to determine who is worthy of inheriting and ruling the kingdom: he challenges every child in the land to grow, in a year's time, the best flower. Already a cracker-jack gardener, Ping inexplicably fails to grow a thing, despite his best efforts. Because the emperor had cooked every seed he distributed, knowing none would grow, he rewards Ping for his honesty and gives him the proverbial keys to the kingdom. *The Empty Pot* aids in promoting understanding in young children of the prosocial value of honesty.

Before You Read Together

The cover holds its share of mysteries. Discuss these questions with your preschooler: Which gender is the child? What kind of clothes are these? Where is the character taking the pot? With what will it be filled? The plot and particular words are more challenging than most preschool fare. Offer preliminary information so that the child understands the premise:

> *This story takes place far away and a long time ago when people wore different clothes. A man called an emperor, which is like a king, was the boss of everyone. He was very rich and very old. He wanted someone to take over his job. How would he pick the right person to take his place? How would he know who was good enough to be his successor— the one who comes next? Who would get to sit on his throne? What child deserved to take over his land or kingdom? He decided to see who could grow the best flower. A boy named Ping, already a good gardener, might have a chance to win!*

After You Read Aloud

- Recall the meanings of new words: *emperor, successor, kingdom, throne*. Use them during dramatic play, with cape and crown, or in conversations. Many children feel proud to know a fancy word's meaning.
- Pull out a puppet after a reading. Pretend that the puppet is disappointed to have missed hearing the story. Have the puppet ask the child to retell it. Check for understanding.
- Is Ping an unusual name to the child? Explore names common in other cultures.

Nothing But the Truth?

Here's the honest-to-goodness truth: A child of preschool age cannot be expected to embrace honesty for its own sake. At this early stage of moral development, experts report that children who generally tell the truth will, nonetheless, lie to avoid punishment or to please another and fit in. In other words, preschoolers lie for self-serving purposes.

Therefore, it isn't so surprising that all the children but Ping substituted seeds in order to:

- ✱ Avoid the emperor's potential displeasure (or punishment);
- ✱ Gain the goodies;
- ✱ Please their parents; and
- ✱ Prove themselves to be the best in the land—the ultimate index for fitting in.

Preschoolers actually may believe something to be "true" because for them, wishing makes it so. Or they may lie because they've decided that honesty isn't always the best policy. If they make a mistake and face a grown-up who is likely to punish them, they are apt to decide that there's no gain in inviting pain. They'll try to protect themselves from feeling shame. The asset related to truth telling among the preschool set reflects awareness of this early stage. What can you do to encourage honesty?

- ✱ Make it "safe" to tell the truth.
- ✱ Offer reminders: "We believe in speaking the truth in our family (in this classroom)."
- ✱ Examine and change adult habits that children may copy—white lies, frequent exaggeration, falsehoods communicated beyond the family or between parents and providers or teachers.

Even a grown-up's expressed disappointment with a dishonest statement or act can wound children. Adults can say, "I don't like for you to lie," while making sure to remind preschoolers that they are still loved. Pairing correction or guidance with loving support and expressing trust that they'll do better next time are crucial.

Seeds! Seeds! Seeds!

Stories plant seeds, with curiosity and creative extensions in the world the happy result! Over time, collect seeds from kitchen and garden (e.g., cantaloupe, watermelon, green pepper, cucumber, apple, lima beans, mimosa), the spice rack (poppy, mustard, celery seeds), farm fields (corn, pumpkin, sunflower), and store (birdseed, seed packets, rice grains, popcorn). To avoid introducing mold, thoroughly dry the seeds on a tray or cookie sheet indoors. Then sort and store the seeds in egg carton sections, labeling each type on the carton lid. Use them for:

* Mosaic Art: You'll need plastic tub lids, glue, and different seeds; cotton swabs are optional. Spread a thin layer of glue inside the lid tops. Kids can place the seeds on top of the glue in any pattern or design. (Older children can lightly dip the end of a cotton swab in glue, using this end to pick up a seed and place it glue-side down on the lid base.)

* Edibles: Open a pumpkin. Rinse and toss 1½ cups of seeds in 2 teaspoons of melted butter with salt to taste. Roast the seeds in a single layer on a baking sheet at 300°F for 45 minutes. Cool and enjoy. If possible, show what sunflower seeds look like with the shells on and as parts of a real sunflower. Then snack on the sunflower seeds that come without shells. Show preschoolers that people also eat the tiny seeds that grow on the outside of strawberries.

* Let a preschooler sort the seeds by color or arrange them in order of size.

* Print numbers from 1 to 12 on cards, one number to each card, and invite a child to place the correct number of seeds on the matching numeral.

* Experiment by filling three Styrofoam cups with soil, leaving about an inch of space at the top. Into each cup, sprinkle a pinch of birdseed, followed by a final layer of soil. Draw a sun on one

cup and keep it in a sunny place in your home. Don't water it. Draw water drops on the second cup and water it regularly in a dark place. Draw sun and water on the third, keeping it watered in the sun. See what happens to each over time. You can also plant one kind of uncooked and cooked seeds.

* Place varied seeds in small plastic storage containers with lids. Use as rhythm instruments.
* Read other books about seeds: *The Tiny Seed* by Eric Carle; *Planting a Rainbow* by Lois Ehlert.

Process, Not Product

In your child's life, is the gold star celebrated more than the getting there? There's a fine line between nudging children to try new things and pushing them to measure up or excel. While it's important to over-estimate rather than underestimate what any child is capable of, a family or preschool that condones criticism or even good-natured teasing about less-than-perfect products can stamp out creativity. Imagination requires the freedom to take risks.

A lost treasure at our house is a postcard Mr. Rogers, *the* Mr. Rogers of public TV fame, once sent my 3-year-old son. Kai was a frequent visitor to the television neighborhood. One day I asked if he'd like me to send Mr. Rogers one of his drawings. Kai said yes. The drawing he chose was like the rest of his artwork at the time. Compared to his big sister Liv's large, colorful pictures, Kai's were microscopic. He typically concentrated his tiny, abstract, black scribbles on a fraction of any sheet of paper.

I said nothing about the possibility of a reply. I suspected that Fred Rogers received love offerings by the truckload. Soon after, to the aston-ishment of our family, a postcard addressed to Kai arrived in the mail. The typewritten message, with his typos corrected by hand, came from Mr. R. himself. He did not gush and say "Wow!" or "Fabulous!" or "Good Work!" Instead, he told Kai how thankful he was to have one of his drawings. Though I've forgotten the exact words, he mentioned some-thing very specific about the effort.

In other words, he validated the process and the 3-year-old, without evaluating the product. It wasn't important for the drawing to be *the best* or *better than* someone else's. It wasn't necessary for it to look like or be anything in particular. Soon after, Kai's process expanded and his art exploded. He transformed the sidewalk with rainbow-colored chalk creations. He put pencil to paper on placemats at restaurants. He filled sketch pads. He drew and drew and drew.

"You did your best," Ping's father tells him, "and your best is good enough to present to the Emperor." Kai's best, it turns out, was good enough to present to Mr. Rogers. From a vital tiny seed, much can blossom.

Positive-Values Bonus Best Bets

- **Arnie and the Stolen Markers** by Nancy Carlson. New York: Viking Kestral, 1987.

- **Building a Bridge** by Lisa Shook Begay. Flagstaff, AZ: Rising Moon-Northland, 1993.

- **Dogger** by Shirley Hughes. New York: Lothrop, Lee & Shepard Books, 1988.

- **The Lady and the Spider** by Faith McNulty, illustrated by Bob Marstall. New York: HarperCollins, 1987.

- **A Song for Lena** by Hilary Horder Hippely. New York: Simon & Schuster Books for Young Readers, 1996.

- **10 Minutes till Bedtime** by Peggy Rathmann. New York: Puffin, 2004.

- **Visiting Day** by Jacqueline Woodson, illustrated by James E. Ransome. New York: Scholastic Press, 2002.

☺ Social Competencies

☺ *The assets in this category reflect the importance of inter-personal interactions, of resistance practice, of skills that foster friendship in a world rich in diversity, and of skills that foster peace in a wider world rife with conflict. It's about planning and decision making for preschoolers, but as important, by preschoolers who savor a growing sense of being competent, not to mention content with who they are.*

• •

It is crucial that both girls and boys see themselves reflected in the books they love. A child often will pay more attention to a story that mirrors his people, her culture, and familiar aspects of family life. Sometimes, unwittingly, adults forget to honor this essential element when introducing books.

Particularly when children of a specific color or culture are not part of one's neighborhood or preschool, a grown-up may overlook books in which they appear. Missing from the pages of the books we share and not incorporated as part of an inclusive circle, these children, in real life, can come to represent the unfamiliar or "alien other," rather than potential friends. Thus, children benefit from meeting a diverse group of characters with varying abilities, expanding the human circle or family. Such introductions smooth the way for future meaningful, multicultural connections.

Take an inventory of the books you and other adults choose for your child—whether checked out from the library, given as gifts, or made available at preschool. Do you discover a tendency to choose titles with main characters of the same gender as the young listener? Or the same as the adult reader? Make sure you move beyond stereotypical portraits to celebrate resourceful characters of both genders.

Also included among social competencies are healers and helpers. Such books articulate feelings the child does not yet possess the words to express. The healing stories deal with universal emotions. They reflect challenges common to this age group, encourage empathy, and reveal possible solutions.

Each Living Thing

by Joanne Ryder, illustrated by Ashley Wolff. San Diego: Gulliver Books/
Harcourt, 2000.

IN VERSE, the author describes a world of creatures and makes a plea
for readers to respect and care for them. At the same time, the illustrator shows a multicultural mix of children both aware (and appropriately wary) of wild creatures, such as bears, jellyfish, or alligators. As
the Developmental Assets framework directs, these children show a
sense of danger appropriate to their expanding sense of self and environmental knowledge. The children also actively watch out for those
critters that need their protection, such as ants building towers. While
a naturalist might object to the child on a raised walkway snapping
a picture of an alligator, a reptile with the power to leap up and snap
back, the book is more realistic than most about the wild. *Be aware of
them,* the text reads: *Take care of them. / Be watchful. / Let them be.*

Before You Read Together

For many preschoolers, the girl and dog on the cover, together exploring the life in a tide pool, present an exotic scene. Indeed, they are
likely to prompt more questions than predictions, especially from
3-year-olds, who love asking why and what about almost everything.
How many living things can you count together on the cover that wraps
around the back of the book? How many are familiar? Take a peek at
settings from backyards to nature preserves where domesticated animals and wild things can be found. This introduction may well lead you
to factual picture books that provide more information about the creatures themselves.

After You Read Aloud

- After several readings, see if the child can supply an adjective that describes what kind of worms or snails or bees the author introduces, and be sure to explore together what actions words such as *wriggling* and *darting* and *snapping* describe.
- Find the combinations of words that begin with the same sounds (*circling in the sea; lurch and leap; hooting, hunting*). This builds awareness of distinctions between different sounds.
- After multiple encounters with the book, invite the child to chime in on familiar rhyming words or a verse.

Wild Things

The great wide world beckons, even if it extends only around the block or over the next hill for the child. What are you waiting for? Together:

- Look for animal footprints on moist ground or snow.
- After a rain, whether near a creek or a curbside, follow a leaf or a twig downstream.
- Through the seasons, keep a running record of "firsts." Advise a child of items to look for as seasons change. Let her report sightings of first buds, a first robin, a first fall-colored leaf.
- Enjoy a picnic at sunrise either at lakeside, riverside, or a park. Take time to observe the wildlife.
- Watch the tide come in. When it goes out, discover what stays behind.
- Take a short hike. Stop once or twice along the way to ask a few questions about an object found in nature along the way.
- In each of several lunch bags, place one natural object, such as a river rock, a pinecone, or a twig. Each day choose one to examine, noting its colors, shadows, smell, and texture. Put the object under the faucet and observe how the object changes when it's wet. What sound does it make when shaken in a box? What does its outline look like when drawn? Is there a new use or a special place for it?
- Mimic the movements and sounds of various animals.
- Visit a zoo or an aquarium. "Adopt" a zoo animal or a whale.
- Encourage the child to register for a preschool-level class at a nature center. If you're a parent, encourage participation in a junior naturalist program for his age level when visiting a state park.

* Ramble in woods or along the seashore. Walk in a light rain shower. In boots, deliberately tramp through puddles. In bare feet, sample grass or squishy-squashy mud.
* Visit a "pick-your-own" farm or orchard and handpick apples, strawberries, or oranges.
* Lie on your backs on a grassy slope and take in all of the living, breathing world.

Collections

I once heard the noted psychologist Jean Houston tell about her friend-ship, as a small child, with Pierre Teilhard de Chardin. She did not know at the time that he was a famous philosopher, paleontologist, and priest, but she sensed that he was a special human being.

On their weekly strolls in the park, he would invariably stop here or there to quietly address a rock. He confided to her that if one was patient and open and able to really listen, it was reasonable to expect an answer. Houston admitted that the information he shared and the con-viction with which he relayed it had seemed most natural. His admission freed her to enrich her perceptions of the world around and within her.

The admission comforted and freed me, too—I'm a longtime listener for the proverbial "Yo!" from the universe. Our family hasn't chosen a Christmas tree without pausing to see which one seems to call out to us, and on annual visits to local greenhouses for spring plants, the kids used all their senses to decide which blooms were meant for the cart. Showing a neighbor his collection of prized stones once, my 5-year-old son plucked several in particular from his basket. "These are the ones that called out to me," he said matter-of-factly.

Attentive to what is of special interest to the child, you might en-courage building a first collection with something in the natural world. Does she invariably pluck a special stone or stray feather on walks? Are elephants his favorite animal? (I'm not suggesting you bring home an elephant. Figurines and plush elephants will do.) Would she like taking pictures of flowers with a disposable camera or pressing them in an album? Find a focus and start your search.

The child may be content with a small basket for special stones or delight in displaying specimens (to which you've glued craft store mag-nets) on a cookie sheet. Feathers can be stuck in a square of netting, shells in a plastic fishbowl, and photos in a scrapbook.

Talking about a collection with caring grown-ups and youth builds positive identity. It expands awareness of the world and a caring adult's awareness of a child's unique interests.

Life and Death

Animals in the wild as well as pets provide many preschoolers their first experience with death. A bird may strike a window and die suddenly. Or you may come upon a dead bird during a casual walk. A child may show interest in the still, stiff body and be eager to see a bird's features close-up. He may express sadness that the bird died, exploring what death means through ceremony and play, as in the classic *The Dead Bird* by Margaret Wise Brown.

Surely there will be questions and more intense emotions with the death of any family pet. The Web site for the Humane Society of the United States (www.hsus.org) includes advice for people of all ages dealing with such loss. The organization notes that everyone deserves permission to express grief and any other emotions that the death evokes.

You, the caring grown-up, can use the event as an opportunity to invite questions. For the first time the child may realize that even you do not have all the answers. Simplistic ones—the angels took Buddy away, God wanted Pippi—often add to children's fears and confusion. It's important to acknowledge this passing as one of the great mysteries.

A child may feel guilty for not having paid enough attention to a pet, for not having been sufficiently caring. If an animal dies in its sleep, a preschooler may grapple with fears that he or other loved ones will not wake up from sleeping. For one reason or another, the child may have wished the animal were not around and may worry now that her wish had caused the death. As Mr. Rogers assured children time and again, wishing doesn't make it so. The child needs reassurance that almost everyone has fears and guilty feelings when a loved one dies. Equally important is the assurance that most humans live to be very old and won't die for a long, long time.

Expressing feelings and sharing recollections provide sources of reassurance and comfort. Books also can be springboards for further discussion. Three helpful stories on this topic are *Goodbye Mousie* by Robie H. Harris, *Always and Forever* by Alan Durant, and *The Tenth Good Thing about Barney* by Judith Viorst.

Bein' with You This Way

by W. Nikola-Lisa, illustrated by Michael Bryant. New York: Lee & Low Books, 1994.

CHILD MAGAZINE CALLED THIS BOOK "multicultural literature at its best." *School Library Journal* proclaimed it an "ode to the beauty of diversity." The *San Francisco Chronicle* dubbed it "a rap poem with rich, catchy phrases . . . a wonderful children's anthem." At a playground, an exuberant young child invites a willing group of playmates of all ages to celebrate their uniqueness as they make their moves, do their thing, and acknowledge physical differences and the fact that, nonetheless, at the core, they (and we) are the same. All in all, the high-spirited verse illustrates what social competencies are about—interpersonal skills, self-regulation, cultural awareness and sensitivity.

Before You Read Together

You just know you're in for a good time when you glance at this cover with kids of all ages out and about. The leader of the pack, no more than 5 or 6, in a bright orange shirt, smiles back at you as if to invite your young companion and you to join in. In the top right-hand corner is a mom holding a toddler—someone invariably present as these kids make their way from one playground attraction to the next.

After You Read Aloud

- Talk about opposites: straight and curly, light and dark, thick and thin, long and short, big and little. Ask the child with which of these opposites she identifies. Ask which ones change depending on the circumstance (a child can be big in relation to a baby sibling or little in relation to a parent).
- Celebrate delightful "big" words to trip on the tongue. Together explore their meanings.

- Encourage the child, after a few readings, to supply a missing opposite or a rhyming word by pausing to let her guess what fits. Encourage him to join in on familiar parts. Give a hand signal to indicate when "Ah-ha!" can be "read" or called out in unison.
- Tape-record the entire text or the closing pages when the whole crew jumps and jives to verses that begin with *be-bop-a-doo-bop*. You and the child can mimic some of the characters' moves. Or make up your own.

Lots of Ways to Be

Different—
Mm-mmm,
but the same,
Ah-ha!

Invite the child, along with one or two friends, to make this recipe. It features cookies that are essentially the same because they share the same primary ingredients, but they're also uniquely appealing because of the addition of different ingredients. Allow each child to pick one favorite variation or, if you are making these only with one child, let him choose three. Divide the basic dough (condensed milk and peanut butter) into thirds and ask the child to select and add a different ingredient for each.

RUBY'S SIX-WAY COOKIES

One 14-ounce can condensed milk
1/2 cup peanut butter

1. Preheat oven to 350°F.
2. Make a dough with the condensed milk and peanut butter.
3. Divide the dough into thirds, and mix into each portion ONE of the following ingredients:
   2 cups raisins
   2 cups cornflakes
   3 cups coconut
   2 cups bran flakes
   1 cup chopped nuts or
   2 cups chopped dates
4. Drop by spoonfuls on a greased baking sheet. Bake for 10 minutes.
5. Remove from cookie sheet at once. Regrease cookie sheet for every batch. Cool and serve.

As you taste and test the results, observe that one person's idea of "the best" may be different from another's. It's the variety of possibilities, the differences, that enrich us.

Movers and Shakers

Playgrounds are catchalls for the rhymes and games passed on from generation to generation of children. With adult supervision, young children can observe movers and shakers of various ages, inspiring their own age-appropriate efforts and friendly interactions. With luck, the playground of choice mirrors the diverse cultures, making the child comfortable with the physical differences between playmates. Playgrounds are the training ground for peaceful coexistence.

In addition to engaging with the play equipment available at most playgrounds, preschoolers enjoy indoor or outdoor activities that build large motor skills such as:

* Walking along wooden planks on the ground or floor.
* Jumping a number of times in and out of a hula hoop.
* Chasing and breaking bubbles as someone blows them in the air.
* Hopping or jumping within a maze created by two parallel lines of duct tape.
* Crawling under chairs, through large open-ended cartons, or through a cloth play tunnel.
* Using a large ball to knock down plastic soda pop bottles capped and partially filled with water.
* Dropping objects such as clothespins or Legos into a bottle or narrow container.
* Playing Follow the Leader, with participants taking turns in the lead, demonstrating movements such as jumping, hopping, tiptoeing, marching, baby-stepping, giant-stepping, crawling, walking backward, skipping (for older children), and twirling.
* Mimicking grown-up yoga postures and practicing child-appropriate versions.
* Playing familiar childhood games such as Duck, Duck, Goose; London Bridge Is Falling Down; Ring-around-the-Rosy; and Hide-and-Seek.

The More We Get Together

Children ages 2 and 3 years old begin noticing differences in skin color if they have not already come to realize such differences within their own families. Following are ways to help the child to appreciate diversity:

* Be open to a child's questions. You can pull scientific answers about melanin (skin pigmentation), geography, and family history from *All the Colors We Are/Todos los Colores de Nuestra Piel* by Katie Kissinger. And you can celebrate stories about such differences in books like *The Colors of Us* by Karen Katz, *Black is brown is tan* by Arnold Adoff, and *Whoever You Are* by Mem Fox.

* Introduce the child to songs that reflect another culture or that are sung in another language. The lullaby "Frère Jacques/Are You Sleeping?" is familiar to most. Expand the repertoire with tapes or CDs such as Ella Jenkins's *Multicultural Children's Songs,* José-Luis Orozco's *Diez Deditos,* a collection like *Children of the World,* or certain selections of popular albums like Raffi's *Let's Play.* All are available at www.lakeshorelearning.com.

* Focus on your child's family history, ethnicity, and countries of origin. Familiarize your child with traditional foods, artifacts, music, and customs that people still enjoy today.

* Focus on the culture of a new friend or a culture/country represented in the community. Let the child become an "expert" through concrete, hands-on experiences. Sample the music and folklore. Taste one or more foods common to the place of origin. Attend a festival or crafts fair. Encourage dramatic play about the place and people. Available for such pretend play is multicultural play clothing such as the Vietnamese *ao dai,* the Guatemalan *toto* and *camisa,* the Ghanaian *dashiki* and *kuka,* and others. (See "Resources" on page 224 for information on where to find multicultural play clothing.)

* In your child's bedroom or a group play space, rotate pictures of a range of people and places.

* Each week, say hello in a different language: the Swahili *jambo* (jahm-boh), the Arabic *salaam* (sah-lamn), the Mandarin *ni hao* (nee ha-OW), and the Spanish *hola* (oh-lah). Repeat the greeting all week.

The Ugly Vegetables

• •

by Grace Lin. Watertown, MA: Talewinds/Charlesbridge, 1999.

AN OBSERVANT CHILD notes the differences between her mother's gardening methods and those of the neighbors. She's also dismayed by the contrast between the neighbors' beautiful flower gardens and her mother's Chinese vegetables, which the daughter finds ugly. The child's perspective changes, however, when her mother makes a wonderful soup with the vegetables and neighbors show up to enjoy some, too. Her discomfort about gardening differences changes to delight. Growing in assets, this child overcomes frustrations, uses friendship skills, identifies the emotions she's feeling, celebrates diversity, and comes to appreciate her own unique heritage.

Before You Read Together

A woman and a girl happily tend a patch of earth where small green shoots sprout from the soil. In the background others tend patches in the neighborhood. At this early stage, there's no clue that the veggies will turn ugly.

Some children gravitate to this book because the characters on the cover look like them. Some are curious about what is growing, especially because the title tips them off that something isn't up to snuff. Still others like the upbeat nature of the characters or resonate to the idea of gardening. Who ever said that you can't tell a book by its cover? Predicting—from title, cover illustration, and brief text—what lies between covers empowers children, at age 3 or 13, to make educated guesses about whether or not they'll find a story worthy of attention. This skill is important and a useful practice to learn early.

After You Read Aloud

- Once again, an author includes words of another language (Chinese) within the narrative. Show the child the key at the back of the book that describes the exotic vegetables and together pronounce their names. Using the key reinforces awareness that reading is a way to get helpful information. At the same time, here's a reminder of the existence of other languages. Your attempts to correctly pronounce the vegetables' names establishes you as a learner along with the child and models acceptance and curiosity about other ways of doing and saying things.

Garden-Variety Recipes

You can bring this story to life in several ways:

- ✱ Visit a grocery store that sells fresh or canned Chinese vegetables. Then follow the recipe for "Ugly Vegetable Soup" found at the end of the book.
- ✱ Find a simple recipe that requires one or more items you have grown in your own garden or that you purchase at a farmers' market. Invite the child to pour premeasured ingredients and, with your help, grate or cut veggies.
- ✱ Invite neighborhood grown-ups and/or children to bring a specific ingredient or two to your "soup kitchen." (Use a favorite vegetable soup recipe or the one found on the next page.) After reading *Stone Soup,* retold by Jon J. Muth (or another version), make your own magic. With nothing more than a single *prewashed* stone (large enough so that no one can swallow it) and water, watch how everybody's contributions enrich the pot, just as different people enrich the neighborhood.

SOUP

1. Let the children wash the vegetables.
2. Carefully supervise the cutting of vegetables (already cut in half) into bite-size pieces.
3. An adult can partially cook the carrots and potatoes in a small amount of water over medium heat for 20 minutes or until vegetables are almost tender. Or preschoolers can bring the precooked item.

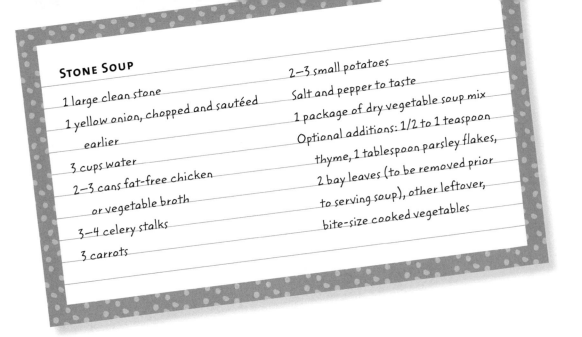

STONE SOUP

1 large clean stone
1 yellow onion, chopped and sautéed earlier
3 cups water
2–3 cans fat-free chicken or vegetable broth
3–4 celery stalks
3 carrots
2–3 small potatoes
Salt and pepper to taste
1 package of dry vegetable soup mix
Optional additions: 1/2 to 1 teaspoon thyme, 1 tablespoon parsley flakes, 2 bay leaves (to be removed prior to serving soup), other leftover, bite-size cooked vegetables

4. Put the stone and water into the pot.
5. Invite participants each to play the part of a villager willing to add the ingredients listed and any others they've brought.
6. An adult can bring the soup to a boil, then turn down the heat. After the soup simmers for about 40 minutes, a grown-up can remove the pot from the heat.
7. Serve the soup in individual bowls, accompanied by oatmeal crackers (or muffins) made while the soup cooks.

CRACKERS

1. Preheat oven to 350°F.
2. Mix ingredients.
3. Roll out dough with rolling pin (thin for crunchy, thick for chewy).
4. Let kids cut the dough into squares, using a plastic knife.
5. Bake until light, golden brown. Cool. Spread jam or preserves on top, if desired.

SUSAN'S OATMEAL CRACKERS

2 cups flour
2 cups quick oatmeal
1/2 cup liquid shortening
1 teaspoon salt
4 teaspoons baking powder
1/2 cup (or more to taste) sugar
1 egg
Milk—enough to moisten dough to rolling consistency

"Berry" Neighborly

One of the rituals that my daughter and I remember fondly was our annual visit to a berry farm in the company of another mom and daughter. We'd dress in old clothes and leave at the crack of dawn. Working down the rows, we'd try our best to put more berries in our boxes than we ate. Sometimes the girls would retrieve refreshments to sip in the shade. Before the sun climbed too high in the sky, the farmer weighed our harvest. We felt triumphant as we poured the berries into their containers.

We had none of the challenges of gardeners fighting weeds or keeping rabbits away, but we did face the same dilemma of any who grow a bumper crop of zucchini or tomatoes—how to use the fruit all at once. Marathon-style, I plunged into making strawberry jam, pies, and frosted strawberry squares, and washing and packaging berries for the freezer.

A friend solved this dilemma and won the goodwill of her neighbors, to boot. You might try this in your own neighborhood. Each June she announces her coming date with a berry patch. Within hours of picking, she sets up chairs and tables on her front lawn and welcomes neighbors to join her. She offers bowls, berries, spoons, and ice cream. Others bring cookies, iced tea, and whipped cream to the summer celebration.

Different but the Same

The young narrator in *The Ugly Vegetables* finds the crop in the backyard strange looking. The fronds freak her out. Those lopsided leaves are losers compared to the other kids' captivating blooms. The main thing is they're different.

The just-turned-4-year-old is as sensitive and observant as any self-conscious teen. The knowing 5-year-old is busy figuring out who fits in, who plays by the rules. Even the 3-year-old begins to calculate what's different. And the difference can make a child uncertain, even fearful.

"Why is your skin that color?" a child may ask a perfect stranger. Unsure of the norm and unschooled in variations on a theme of being human, a preschooler may point and wonder aloud, "How come he can't walk?" An otherwise personable preschooler teases, "You're fat!" or "You dress funny!"

Vulnerability, not cruelty, is talking. Take the time to respond, to inform, and to reassure. Possible responses include:

* "People come in all shapes and sizes. It's okay to be little.
  It's okay to be big."
* "It hurts people's feelings when we laugh or point. How would
  you feel if someone made fun of you?"
* "Girls and boys can do many different things and look many
  different ways and still be just fine as girls and boys."
* "It's fun to laugh *with* someone about something silly that you
  both enjoy. It's not okay to laugh *at* someone who doesn't mean
  to be funny. That kind of laughter hurts."
* "We have different skin colors/she's deaf/he can't see for a
  reason. Let's find out why."

They see that we accept differences—our own and others'. We affirm
tolerance and human kindness as the way to go, to grow. Sooner or later,
they see, as the young gardener does, that beauty is truly in the eye of
the beholder. That it's only skin-deep, anyway. That being a caring and
confident member of the melting pot can be downright delicious.

This Is Our House

by Michael Rosen, illustrated by Bob Graham. Cambridge, MA: Candlewick Press, 1996.

IN AN AUTHOR'S NOTE, Michael Rosen writes: "Our attitudes about who's okay and who's not get formed when we're very young. I've watched how some children carve out a space for themselves using the language of discrimination. This book is a way of looking at that." Basing his decisions on physical differences, one child excludes others from play in a large cardboard carton. It's a simple depiction of playground dynamics that *Kirkus Reviews* called "surprisingly powerful" and about which *Publishers Weekly* proclaimed, "Every word rings true." The story highlights problem solving, peaceful coexistence, and conflict resolution.

Before You Read Together

Nine children surround a carton painted with flowers, window frames, and rooftop squiggles. On the back cover, the group applies lots of tape to restore the battered playhouse to its original shape. What questions do these introductory illustrations raise for the child you're reading with? Some questions to talk about include: Can all the children fit in one box? Do they plan to use it as a garage for the car that's pictured? How else could they use it? Do they all want to do the same thing in and with the carton?

After You Read Aloud

- The story provides an opportunity for the child to talk with you about personal experiences related to sharing personal belongings as well as jointly owned playthings. Talk about what makes it hard to share. Ask if the companionship of playing with another is worth the effort to share.

- The first pages make it clear that all the characters claim the found object that they are dragging. Does the child possess a concept of fairness? Is it clear to her that George does not own the carton? Is there anybody who the child thinks should stay out? If so, explore why.
- Explore a "what if." What if George did own the carton? If he didn't share, what would happen? Would playing alone be as much fun? Since everybody wants to play, can the preschooler solve the problem of too many people in the carton at once?

Carton to Castle

Take one box and one boy or girl and watch what happens. Give children a chance to play with a large, plain appliance box and any number of transformations occur. Most are happy to play with it as is. If asked, cut out a few well-placed openings or apply paint, but avoid getting hung up on the final result. Let the child make the creative decisions.

For our 3-year-old daughter, we transformed a carton into a "stone" castle, thanks to brushes and black paint. Two years later, I found myself lugging another oversized carton into her kindergarten room where a popular puppet had inspired children to perform their own shows. A large opening in one side and, on the side opposite, an entry door created by cutting three sides of a rectangle were all we needed for a roomy theater that accommodated a few kids at a time.

Given advance notice, a manager of a store that sells appliances is apt to be open to setting aside a shipping carton for pickup by you instead of the trash collector. At home, brainstorm with the child about the carton's potential uses. If the desire is to crawl around in the box, to roll down a gentle slope while inside it, or to slap different colors of paint on the large surface, let the child lead. Following, however, are common possibilities:

- A tunnel with open ends, bridging one space to another;
- A cave (leave one side open);
- A book nook (add comfortable pillows and books, and let light in from a cutout in the top);
- A vehicle (glue on paper wheels, etc.);
- A castle or cottage; and

* A four-sided prop for dramatic play (on one side a jungle scene, on another a play store with shelves and signs, on the third side a train station ticket booth or puppet stage with open window, and on the last side a barn for toy animals or pretend livestock).

Consider relaying thanks and a photo of child and transformed carton to the storekeeper, making it more likely that a future request from you or another will be welcomed.

Creative Playthings

The last time I found myself in one of those discount toy warehouses I got queasy. It's the sheer volume of cheap, breakable, sometimes abominable playthings that overwhelms me. But then I've been known to break into a sweat peering into any kid's room where the stash of stuff makes it virtually impossible to see the floor or to open the bedroom door.

The characters in *This Is Our House,* on the other hand, live in a sterile wasteland, save for that circle of light and color called the playground. They are like so many kids in the world today, left to their own devices, numbing out in front of the TV. An hour imaginatively spent in an empty box is a rarity. Are there playthings that these children, that every child, should own? Or, as Cynthia Gerdes, founder of Creative Kidstuff (www.creativekidstuff.com) poses the question, "Are there a few essentials for that hypothetical island, with not a DVD in sight?"

Gerdes, who has seen it all, and whose stores are magical environments that lift one's spirits, says, "Yes!" This veteran observer of every gimmick that's come down the pike says all preschoolers, when possible, deserve to have certain basics in their lives. Our expert names five:

1. Wood blocks. Small ones. Big ones. In-between ones. Blocks with a natural finish or in bright colors are some of the most open-ended, wildly creative playthings around.

2. A doll or a stuffed animal for every girl *and* every boy. This plaything encourages nurturing, caregiving, and loving-kindness. It's the perfect imaginative tool/toy for raising kids destined to become loving parents.

3. Dress-up clothes—old clothes, costumes, capes, hats, and the like inspire imaginative play. Put a cape on a kid and watch that child transform magically into someone else!

4. Music. "Raffi still claims my heart . . . even after all these years," says Gerdes. Singing on CDs and tapes, Raffi brings to successive generations of enamored preschoolers delight and wonder. Play music of all kinds, especially before bed. Make this a nightly ritual after reading a book. The child will always remember this special time.

5. Art made from anything. The ultimate open-ended plaything is a collection of art supplies. Self-confidence and creativity blossom as children exercise their imaginations, so keep a box of "art stuff" at the ready—empty toilet paper tubes, glitter, ribbons, used gift-wrap, glue sticks, pipe cleaners. It's the treasure kids go back to again and again!

Take an inventory of home, child-care site, and preschool to see if the fab five rate inclusion in each place. If not, support adding the items, found in thrift stores and at yard sales, requested from relatives for birthdays and holidays, and borrowed from friends or lending libraries. Make a point of giving such creative playthings as gifts and contributions, if you have the means.

Beauty Before Me . . .

No child ought to live in a world without beauty. It is all around, if only we seek and see it. Send children on missions to find beautiful objects of a certain color—creations of the natural world. Accept these offerings with gratitude and a respect for each child's own idea of what constitutes beauty. Try these other ways to engage all of a child's senses:

* Call attention to things such as a bird song, chiming bells, awe-inspiring music, or voices. Play a tape recording of frogs in a marsh or water gurgling in a stream during quiet time.

* Store objects with pleasing textures in an accessible basket or box, including swatches of velvet, satin, fur, and fleece. Together, celebrate the feel of silky blanket edging, a smooth piece of beach glass, or a kitten's soft fur. Introduce textured alphabet letters of sandpaper, rubber, or wood.

* Bring "scentsational" additions into a child's daily experience: a container of fragrant lilacs; an apple pie fresh-baked from the oven; cotton balls soaked in popular essences, such as vanilla or peppermint.

* Periodically provide favorite foods freshly picked or made from scratch, in contrast to monotonous servings of packaged, processed, microwaved, or fast food. Survey people's favorite tastes, picking a new one to sample each day. Introduce words such as *sour* and *sweet*.

* Visually enrich and enliven each space where a child spends part of each day. Mount one or more posters, laminated for durability. While art geared for children is a frequent choice, don't ignore museum reproductions. In contemporary or abstract art, for example, the forms and colors alone are beautiful. Kandinsky's *Squares with Concentric Circles,* Van Gogh's *Starry Night,* and Klee's *With the Eagle* are three possibilities. (See "Resources" on page 224 for information on where to find a wide range of art posters.)

* Introduce order and harmony to a child's bedroom with sensible storage, calming wall colors, a small plant, a nature table on which to rotate treasures, or a bulletin board with picture postcards of beautiful places in the world. How many features of the preschooler's classroom bring beauty into the mix? How can each corner inspire, soothe, or delight? When you look at your child's surroundings, each place where children spend their days, be proactive, mindful of the Navajo night chant:

With beauty behind me I walk
With beauty above me and about me, I walk,
It is finished in beauty
It is finished in beauty.

When Sophie Gets Angry— Really, Really Angry . . .

by Molly Bang. New York: The Blue Sky Press/Scholastic, 1999. (Spanish edition: *Cuando Sofía se enoja, se enoja de veras . . .*)

THIS BOOK, which won the Caldecott Honor Medal, shines a spotlight on a child who "roars a red, red roar" with angry feelings. After running, crying, and climbing into her favorite tree where "the wide world comforts her," Sophie feels better enough to head back to her family's embrace. It's a prompt for talking about stages and ways of dealing with a universal emotion, and it's a springboard for reinforcing the asset that relates to identifying and self-regulating feelings.

Before You Read Together

The eyes have it: dots of intense blue surround ink black pupils that tell us Sophie is not a happy camper. Does the child have a word to describe this facial expression on the cover? Talk about times when people might get mad or angry. Explain how the word *really* repeated twice suggests that Sophie is feeling more anger than usual. Invite the preschooler to guess what Sophie does when she gets so angry. Paraphrase Mr. Rogers's famous question put into song and ask, "What do *you* do with the mad inside whenever you feel it?" Mention that all of us feel mad sometimes and that all of our feelings are natural aspects of being human.

After You Read Aloud

- Make it clear that Sophie runs and runs as a way of letting the mad feelings out, but that she isn't running away. She is removing herself from the situation until she feels better.

- It's hard for most preschoolers to climb a tree. Sophie's tree looks easy to climb. Most people don't have such a tree, and preschoolers cannot travel too far away from the place where they get angry. Can the child problem-solve with you about alternatives?
- The artist outlines the main character Sophie in red while she is filled with anger. Does the child notice that as Sophie works through the explosive feelings, the color of her outline changes? By story's close, the parents, Sophie (who had a yellow outline at first), and her sister (who had a green outline as she coveted a toy) have yellow outlines now. They're happy.

Art Therapy

Talk about colors and the feelings associated with them. Green can be a sign to some of peaceful calm, reminding them of nature. Or green can represent jealousy ("green with envy"). What feelings does the preschooler associate with various colors? (You may want to point out swatches of colored paint chips, construction paper, or fabrics as you ask for feedback.) There are no right answers. He may take his cues about colors and feelings from this story. She may associate a feeling and color with a past event where that color predominated. A child can feel differently about associations only hours or a week later.

When it comes to the preschool set, emphasize *process*. The objective of this next activity is to enjoy the process of gluing and then using the marker, not to produce observable facial expressions or identifiable objects. Affirmations can be specific: "You are really concentrating." "What a happy, peaceful color." If the child wants to work in stages or on a smaller scope (using one color group or one feeling), follow the little one's lead. You'll need:

☐ Colored tissue paper
☐ Black permanent marker
☐ Large sheet of paper
☐ School glue diluted with a small amount of water
☐ Brush (optional)

Have fun tearing up different sizes and shapes of colored tissue paper. Encourage the child to group colors that are similar (various blues or red and orange). Let the child submerge each piece in the glue solution and place it on the sheet (or brush the solution onto the sheet and cover it with the tissue). Overlap tissue. Group similar colors associated with different feelings.

Let the sheet dry. Depending on the child's maturity level, encourage use of the black marker to draw lines or shapes or faces or things that seem to go with each color and feeling.

The Red, Red Roar

As young children acquire skills and more words to talk about their feelings, the aggressive behavior observed in toddlers typically diminishes. Nevertheless, it is unrealistic to expect young kids to be cool, calm, and collected at all times. Sometimes their anger is justified.

Squelching or ignoring anger can increase anxiety or lead to later explosive outbursts. It's useful to remind children that anger is human. It helps to give a name to this emotion and to build a vocabulary that shows them how to talk about anger, or any other feeling, for that matter.

Books like this one teach preschoolers to express their feelings in a nonviolent manner. Grown-ups can be sensitive to behavior changes, offering a way to talk things out. You observe a facial expression, a posture, or an action and kindly remark about it: "You are using a grumpy voice; did you have a hard day today?" "Are you mad that your brother left you behind?" "Your eyes tell me it's upsetting for you." "Want to talk about what feeling is inside?" The child may prefer:

* Dramatic play. Encourage her to play out her anger through her toys and to role-play.
* Music. Put on loud, lively music that allows for stomping, jumping, marching, moving.
* A change of scenery. Designate a private space—an empty appliance carton or a corner of the backyard or room—where the child knows he can let his anger cool, reflect on the event, and restore calm, as the character Sophie does.
* Art. On a sidewalk, let her dip a big brush into a pail of water to "paint" wide swooping swaths. Let him paint a red volcano picture. Let her pound some play dough or clay.

Avoid responding to anger in kind. Your explosive or angry response sends a message that throwing tantrums, yelling, or even striking out is the way to deal with anger. Be firm. Problem-solve together. Be a focused listener, repeating back what the child says to assure him that you hear him.

Puppet Power

Cody, who, to my knowledge, never uttered an audible word, won the hearts of many. I have to admit that wherever she appeared, she invariably attracted a crowd and anyone who met her soon called her "friend." Even the shiest held forth in her presence.

Cody was a giraffe. More to the point, she was a giraffe puppet that smoothed the way during read-aloud sessions with preschoolers and kindergartners who liked nothing better than to talk to her about the featured story and about things they wouldn't think of telling the grownups. As the children she knew made the march up the grade-level ladder, they insisted she come along. Second-grade boys jostled to give the bashful giraffe a smooch or a quick hug. Jaded 3rd-graders, already into designer jeans, asked if Cody could visit again, please. It was something to behold.

Somehow a puppet remains independent of the hand over which it rests—even if the attached grown-up's lips are babbling "Puppetese," even if the voice sounds like Mama's. Puppets can help the tongue-tied and the terribly shy to speak up. They may invite young children to express a frustration or to confide safely a source of anger. Miffed or mad themselves, puppets can show how to express and deal with such emotions, besides being a whole lot of fun.

The size of inexpensive finger puppets makes this type much easier for preschoolers to manipulate. They're a perfect prop for story extensions—the white mouse that scampers across the page from word to word, a lamb to sing along on "Baa Baa Black Sheep," one that resembles Piggy teaching basic hygiene. (See "Resources" on page 224 for information on where to find book-related finger puppets.)

With a drill press and a jigsaw, my friend Mike created puppet stands for the whole menagerie. Into each circular wood base (8-inch diameter), he glued ¼-inch dowels of varying lengths into seven holes. I spray-painted the stand. The puppets, smiling from their dowel perches, promise a happy time.

Social-Competencies Bonus Best Bets

- **And to Think That We Thought That We'd Never Be Friends**
  by Mary Ann Hoberman, illustrated by Kevin Hawkes. New York:
  Crown, 1999.

- **The Colors of Us** by Karen Katz. New York: Henry Holt, 1999.

- **Goodbye Mousie** by Robie H. Harris, illustrated by Jan Ormerod.
  New York: Margaret K. McElderry Books, 2001.

- **Margaret and Margarita/Margarita y Margaret** by Lynn Reiser.
  New York: Greenwillow, 1993.

- **¡Pío Peep! Traditional Spanish Nursery Rhymes** selected by Alma
  Flor Ada and F. Isabel Campoy, translated by Alice Schertle and
  illustrated by Viví Escrivá. New York: HarperCollins, 2003.

- **Stone Soup** by Jon J. Muth. New York: Scholastic Press, 2003.

- **Whoever You Are** by Mem Fox. San Diego: Voyager/Harcourt, 1997.

Positive Identity

It is not too soon to teach a child about personal power—not power over, but power within—to meet challenges, to make friendships, to keep becoming more and more of what already waits inside, to blossom into fullness. Adults build this positive view of a personal future by supporting and affirming young children's skills and competencies, and helping them explore the world around them. Family members share stories of the past—family history and anecdotes about a child's beginnings. All adults express as well what they love about a child in the present. As the child sets out on an exciting life journey, books offer signposts along the way: possible choices, a preview of challenges to come, and positive solutions. And they offer hope that ultimately, down the road, all will be well.

* *

LITERACY EXPERTS TELL US there's an astonishing correlation between children's readiness or emergent literacy on the first day of kindergarten and their subsequent achievement through 6th grade. What an opportunity is available to adults who know what to do to secure such success for the children they love. Awareness of the predictors of success empowers families, preschool educators, and other caring adults to "take control" and to give young children the right start.

Playful Reading opens a door for relationships like yours to provide a sense of real and transforming personal power for children. The following books in particular feature characters with a positive view of a personal future. May they inspire in real readers—grown-ups and children in loving relationship—a similar sense of pride and purpose.

Con Mi Hermano/ With My Brother

• •

by/por Eileen Roe, illustrations by/ ilustraciones por Robert Casilla. New York: Simon & Schuster Books for Young Readers/Aladdin Paperbacks, 1994.

THIS BILINGUAL STORY features two Latino siblings who are devoted to each other. The preschool-age narrator describes his much-admired big brother's activities—delivering newspapers, playing on a baseball team, going off to school. While this little boy admits that sometimes his brother doesn't have time to play, he's proud to list the many occasions when he does show his love—playing catch, putting a puzzle together, reading favorite books. He tells us: "When he sees me, he smiles and calls my name," and when the big brother jokes that one day the little one will be "too big to sit on his lap," the preschooler consoles himself, thinking that by then maybe he'll be able to do the things this beloved brother already can do. The young child's trust in milestones to come, his sense of personal power, his optimistic view of a personal future, and positive self-esteem wonderfully illustrate this category of assets.

Before You Read Together

Two boys, one little and one big, are clearly enjoying themselves, sharing a ride on a tire swing and, in the back cover illustration, sitting quietly together on the playground's merry-go-round. The title is the tip-off for what's to come. Does the child notice that they have matching caps? Does he or she have any predictions of what the boy does with his brother in this story?

After You Read Together

- Point out that the child (narrator) tells this story in two different languages, English and Spanish. If you or someone you know is proficient in Spanish you may wish to read each page in one language and then, for comparison, the other. At the very least, isolate one or more words to show that they differ in shape, form, sound, and letters. For example, *hermano* is the word Spanish-speaking people use for the English word *brother.* Play with language, introducing in a second language a few words, such as the numbers from 1 to 10, a familiar song such as "Frère Jacques," a phrase, or a greeting *(Ciao! Hola! Adios!)*.

Body Language

Simple gestures—a thumb repeatedly touching one's lips, for example, to signify "drink" or the desire for one—allow babies and toddlers to communicate with any parent or caregiver who understands these signs. *Baby Signs,* developed by authors Linda Acredolo and Susan Goodwyn, is a book about the use of such gestures for objects, feelings, and activities. It's gaining many supporters. The authors' studies, funded by the National Institutes of Health, show a range of benefits—from reduced frustration for tots to increased IQs at school age. Perhaps the preschooler in your life is a veteran of such signing.

Young children in your care may enjoy songs and finger plays like "The Itsy Bitsy Spider," which incorporate gestures that help a child remember the words. And surely the little ones you know and love are experts at "reading" your pleased, puzzled, or perturbed facial expressions—wordless messages that come through loud and clear.

Facial expressions in particular, and body language in general, are especially helpful in settings where this visual language can bridge a communication gap between people who speak different languages. In the English Language Learners (ELL) classroom or at the community sandbox, children and adults can reach out to each other via such visual cues. Heighten a preschooler's awareness and appreciation of body language in the following ways:

- Agree to use some of the pictured hand signs in *Baby Signs,* if you don't already know or use any of them. Create a few of your own signs to use within the family or preschool group.

* In situations that demand quiet, use a set of signs to communicate silently.
* To underscore the power of touch and visual cues with animals, share *Without Words* by Joanne Ryder, with its heartwarming photos of children and diverse critters communicating.
* Engage in simple charades, guessing as each player pretends to be an animal. Invite one or more children to silently dramatize the actions in a familiar story after you read it aloud.
* Introduce older preschoolers to American Sign Language. Beautiful illustrations in Laura Rankin's picture book, *The Handmade Alphabet,* give examples of each letter in the manual alphabet, used by deaf individuals. Figure out how to sign the letters in the preschooler's name. George Ancona and Mary Beth Miller's *Handtalk Zoo* features photos of hands spelling out letters of specific words as well as signs for animals and common words such as *time* and *pizza*.
* Take turns guessing the feeling behind facial expressions you make in a mirror. Provide the words that describe each expression—*surprised, grumpy, angry, sad*.

Tape Players

Allow me to send up a hurrah—in the age of the DVD, the MP3, and the ZIP drive—and praise the lowly audiocassette player. For preschoolers, this humblest of technologies happens to be the handiest of servants. An inexpensive and fairly indestructible one sets the child free!

* Teaching the preschooler to operate a cassette player independently fosters both competence and self-confidence. No substitute for a warm body or the warmth of a read-aloud ritual, it does allow the child to appreciate the finer points of an already familiar book or song multiple times.
* Use of the tape player not only increases the number of exposures to books, but also prompts the child, in the very act of choosing a particular cassette, to look for symbolic cues distinguishing one tape from another.
* When you narrate recordings of favorite books, in a sense you can be present for the child at times when you're apart. The tinkling of a bell or the snap of your fingers signaling time for a page turn and the sound of your voice provide a link to the familiar.

* When you record bedtime rituals—a story, songs, conversations, and "good nights"—the everyday exchanges become, over time, priceless treasures. (We listened recently to a tape of our pre-school-age daughter, Liv, interviewing herself! She describes a special friend as sisterlike. This person is now a young mother, as is our daughter, and the two are still friends today.)

* Commercially produced sets of an audiotape and its companion book are available at public libraries. Featuring actors with mesmerizing read-aloud skills, many now offer bonuses incorporating creative movement, related songs, or background information about the story.

* Tapes of music and books hold special significance for families who speak another first language. Listening repeatedly builds phonemic awareness (the ability to distinguish differences between sounds), an ability that predicts school success for English language learners, even when they don't have optimal oral proficiency. Along with wordless picture books that they "read" in their first language, tapes in English tell a story that the grown-up and child can then talk about in their native tongue. Similarly, tapes with selections in another language enrich English-speaking children's perceptions and expand their horizons.

Connections with Youth

Once, at a workshop, I was searching for an apt description for how preschoolers perceive most youth, and a participant shouted out, "As gods!" The other participants chuckled knowingly and nodded.

A child is fortunate, indeed, if, like the little brother in this story, there's a caring youth in her or his life. Let an older child recognize her or his importance as a role model and as a source of wonder for preschoolers who look up to young people. To foster meaningful connections with the sitter, the teenage cousin, or the older sibling, look for active rather than passive ways to enrich time spent together. Turn off the TV and suggest something spontaneous such as washing a bike or a car. Encourage a familiar ritual with sitters: just after we departed for an evening out, our sitter and kids would make special ice cream sundaes together.

Promote an activity between a teenager and the child that both can enjoy by planning in advance and supplying needed materials. You might try the following:

* Have them interview each other on tape, offering a list of potential questions: "What's your favorite food?" "What makes you happy?" "What's the best thing about being a baby, a preschooler, a teenager?" "What do you like most about me?" Add symbols as cues for the child's list or let the teen ask first, inspiring the younger child's questions. Or alternate who does the questioning.

* Use *Ed Emberley's Fingerprint Drawing Book* for inspiration. Have the two use their own thumbprints to create critters and cartoon-like characters with an ink pad, fine-point marker, and paper. They might invent a story together about the creatures they've created.

The First Thing My Mama Told Me

by Susan Marie Swanson, illustrated by Christine Davenier. San Diego: Harcourt, 2002.

ON HER SEVENTH BIRTHDAY, the main character, Lucy, recounts all the wonderful ways that loved ones, in her brief history, have embraced her name. They have reinforced their love for Lucy, whether squeezing the letters out of a tube of frosting to top a cupcake, painting "LUCY" on a step stool, or printing it on the belongings she retrieves from her school's Lost and Found. This exposure helps to speed Lucy's own attempts at printing her name—with chalk on the front steps or with boots and snow—stomping letters "big enough for the sun and moon to read." In a book that celebrates numerous personal milestones, a loving link to one's own special name offers a sense of personal power and positive self-esteem.

Before You Read Together

Contrast the cover of a fully dressed child at school standing near a coat rack that bears a name and the back of the book where the younger child, in her underwear, scribbles on the floor. These cues may be enough to prompt a correct prediction from your preschooler about the book's content, but don't be surprised if, when you ask the child what the title means, something entirely unexpected comes forth. Then read together to see if the story jibes with the guess.

After You Read Aloud

- After a reading, ask the child what he likes about his name. Does he know other people with the same name? Does he know why it was given? If not, tell or find out how he came to have it.

- Does she go by a nickname or do one or more people call her something else? Tell or find out the story about this bonus name. Later, invite her to explain her understanding of its origins.
- Here's a chance to talk about favorites, such as the child's opinion of the most interesting way Lucy's name materialized on objects in the world. With your own child's name, can you reproduce that favorite use? Ask the child if he or she has another favorite name and playfully use it instead for an hour or for a whole day.

What's in a Name?

If there was ever an advertisement for appreciating the uses or functions of print, this book is it. In many ways, the main character has repeat encounters with a combination of letters that have special meaning for her and the people who love her. Poetically, the author shows ways grown-ups can call attention to the letters in a child's name without resorting to tedious instruction. An entering kindergartner's ability to recognize his name when he sees it, to name most or all of the alphabet letters in it, is one of the predictors for later success at reading for meaning.

Even the way Lucy initially scribbles what she pretends to be her name illustrates the natural learning process. From engaging in playful scribbling to first attempts to correctly copy letter shapes to a close approximation of the actual letters, children learn to print their names, too, and often well before kindergarten. Here are more examples of ways to incorporate print at home:

- Place a sign on the child's bedroom door that bears her name.
- On an object such as a Plexiglas box, a toy license plate, a rock, stationery, a sweatshirt, a mirror, or a backpack print his name with paint, colored marker, embroidery, letter tiles, or stickers.
- Write the child's name on a birthday cake, a Christmas stocking, or a colorful banner.
- Add the child's name to any of her works of art and homemade crafts.
- "Send" postcards and love notes to which you add (and emphasize) his name.
- Personalize pancakes by pouring out each letter's shape first, taking care to form most (B, C, D, E, F, G, J, K, L, N, P, Q, R, S, and Z) backward on the griddle; a few seconds later, cover the letter with

more batter and flip when bubbles form over the surface. There you go—initialed hotcakes. If you're feeling ambitious and can warm waiting cakes in the oven, make enough golden spheres to spell out a whole name. (Alphabet soup and cereal provide other chances to identify and combine letters.)

Glitter and Glue

Brainstorm about positive words that begin with each of the letters in the child's name. A dictionary offers the most candidates. You can include phrases as well. For example, if there is an "e" in the name, a few of the possibilities are energetic, easy to like, embraceable, entertaining, enchanting, extra special, early to rise, enjoyable to be with, enthusiastic, excellent, and easygoing. Avoid negative descriptions, such as exhausting or explosive. Most words will be new and strange to the child. Make sure you explain in simple terms or playfully, with facial expressions and dramatic actions, what the chosen words mean, each a source of curiosity and pride.

On a sheet of construction paper, poster board, or newsprint, in large capital letters lightly print the child's name vertically from top to bottom. Following each first letter, print horizontally the remaining letters of each chosen descriptive word, using lowercase, smaller print, and colored markers. Here's an example:

M ellow
I maginative
K ind
E xtra special

Invite the child to trace the lines of the beginning letter with a glue stick. Help with sprinkling glitter over the glue and shaking off extra glitter before moving on to the next letter in the name. Post this acrostic in a prominent spot, evidence of the preschooler's sparkling personality.

With a younger child, you may simply print the name horizontally with no descriptive words. Follow with glue and glitter. An option at a future date is to cut out squares surrounding each separate letter. Mix up the letters and challenge the preschooler to put them in the order that spells out the name. When little or no assistance is required, praise the feat.

Name That Tune

In our family, the birth of each baby has inspired, soon after, simple songs to supplement the lullabies and nursery rhymes sung to woo the new arrival to sleep. It's a way to acquaint Baby early on with the combination of sounds that signify the given name. And it probably reflects the available time in the early weeks to create such ditties at three in the morning, or whenever the new arrival happens to awaken for some TLC.

The tradition continues with our next generation. In fact, a song that started with a single simple verse featuring the newborn's name and a trait or two the parents hoped would soon appear ("He's a good sleeper . . .") as well as statements of fact ("He's a keeper!") has expanded at last count to at least four verses. The song reflects lovely and loved aspects of this baby's being.

Create just such a song for the preschooler. In fact, the child may want to try out rhyming verses with you, whether the notation matches a familiar song or you make up the tune yourself. The song that celebrates the child and includes the given name may evolve over time, but make sure to jot down the lyrics or perform the tune on tape or video for posterity.

Such songs usually are easy to remember since they seem to resurface when you and the child are sharing happy memories, when you are celebrating a milestone of some kind, or when you are reminding the child of the love that went into the naming. This activity is especially important for children whose names may be difficult for outsiders to pronounce or can be the object of teasing, however good-natured. (One book that features a child self-conscious about her name is *My Name Is Yoon* by Helen Recorvits.) The love song offers a counterpoint to any disadvantages or difficulties related to the name. Having a special song strengthens positive identity.

Taxi! Taxi!

• •

by Cari Best, illustrated by Dale Gottlieb. New York: Orchard Books, 1997.

HERE'S A POSITIVE LOOK at one day in the life of a girl with divorced parents. Highlighted is the time she spends with her nonresident father and the diverse and supportive community of neighbors that Tina and Papi serve when they provide a free ride home in her father's taxi cab. In Tina's world, life is exciting and enjoyable and she has a positive place within it, keys to positive identity.

Before You Read Together

A girl on the cover rides in the front seat of a big yellow taxi, depicted as a child might draw it. Ask why she is sitting in the front seat. Does she know the driver? The title mimics the shout common to those hailing a cab. Pretend that you are on a curb together, getting the attention of a driver by each raising an arm and calling out the words, too: "Taxi! Taxi!"

After You Read Aloud

- Does the child notice that the many words in Tina's chant, beginning "My name is Tina—," start with the same sound? You can isolate the words that all begin with "T" and show the letter form for each, if the child is curious about the look of letters that make the "tuh" sound.
- The Spanish words embedded in the English text give us another clue about the ethnic background of the main characters. Last names often tell a story about ethnicity, too. Does the child's name tell such a story? Does yours?
- Is your child's family like Tina's, including a single parent with whom she resides and one who visits, or is this an unfamiliar dynamic for the preschooler? Make sure your child understands that divorce is not the fault of the children in a family. Allow him

to express feelings (a fear of loss or abandonment; sadness about a situation, whether hers or another's; envy of a child of divorce who frequently gets toys or favors). Welcome the child's questions about why families are different or how divorces come to be. If possible, at home and at preschool, talk positively about children you know who have different family setups and what makes a family a family.

Testing, Testing . . .

Children need to see themselves reflected in the stories they read, and the child of divorce is no exception. In fact, because so many marriages end in divorce, it's a good idea to expose all children to this fact of life for others, if not themselves. Books like *Let's Talk about It: Divorce* by Fred Rogers, *Two Homes* by Claire Masurel, and *A New Room for William* by Sally Grindley offer more opportunities to answer questions and encourage extended talk about the subject. The most intense dynamics, however, often don't make it into picture books.

As Drs. Brazelton and Sparrow point out in *Touchpoints Three to Six,* even a 3-year-old can be aware of an impending separation and attempt to keep her parents together. Young children feel a sense of responsibility for a major event in a family, even when it's clear to the grown-ups that the child hasn't caused it. A single parent needs to remember that the most difficult but powerful task is to foster the child's relationship with the other parent. Preoccupied with anger or grief, par-

CHILD-FRIENDLY DIVORCE

While divorce is never easy for children, this story realistically reflects factors that make it bearable. For the most part, the characters embody the principles that experts recommend on behalf of the child. If Papi occasionally falls short in the dependability department, he is stellar in other respects:

* Papi's time with Tina is focused time. She is the center of his universe while they are together.
* His humorous and loving comments remind Tina that he is happy to be in her company.
* He admits to feeling loneliness at times and permits her to acknowledge such feelings as well.
* He finds opportunities to affirm his daughter, to build positive identity at a time when children typically blame themselves, when identity is shaky.
* He offers a memento of their time together, a symbol during his absence of enduring love.
* He is no stranger to the neighbors, taking time to make a memory that includes them.
* "Let's go upstairs," he tells Tina when they return, an indication that he and her mother interact peaceably. They both have her best interests at heart.
* Neither parent expresses hostility toward the other. Even when Mama might have used Papi's failure to deliver on a promise to proclaim him unfit or unfeeling, she doesn't.

ents with few resources to offer a child during such a transition must actively seek support from extended family, friends, and even neighbors, as in this story.

In books like *The Runaway Bunny* by Margaret Wise Brown and *Mama, Do You Love Me?* by Barbara Joosse, each mother tells the child who tests her love and loyalty that her own love is steadfast. During separation or after divorce, whether a child becomes clingy or continually tests your patience, whether she suffers from nightmares or acts insufferably, whether he is "too good to be true" (fearful of abandonment or hoping to make things better) or too naughty to be believed (projecting the "bad" person he believes has caused the problem), the message that bears repeating is "I won't let you go."

Out-of-home caregivers and parents who are aware of fears or grief that give rise to such testing can better meet children's needs. Be patient with and supportive of the child acting out or acting differently. Remind a child of divorce that she bears no responsibility for problems in the marriage—for fights or the final parting. Repeatedly assure him of your and others' continuing love. The constancy of rules and routines will make him feel more secure, too.

When Life Hands You Lemons

"I wish you lived with me and Mama. Then I could see you every day," Tina tells Papi.

On the way home, they pass a family with a mama, a *papi,* and a little girl. "I have two families," Tina thinks. "Papi and me. And Mama and me."

Tina makes the best of an imperfect situation. Despite past disappointments, she is resilient. She knows she is lovable. ("For my best girl," her father says.) She knows she is loved. And not only by her parents. She is lucky to have all kinds of neighbors—Mr. Morelli, Anita and her mother and the baby, Mrs. Sweeney, Mr. Henry, and Mr. Salazar—who appreciate her.

Tina misses her papa. The neighbors are a kind of extended family whose presence makes what could be a bitter experience sweeter. Imagine how happy they would be to return the favor of the free ride and patronize Tina's lemonade stand. Think of the opportunities this presents for encouraging friendly chatter, for building positive identity, for making life a bit sweeter on your block. You'll need:

- Lemonade (recipe below)
- Paper cups
- Ice cubes
- A small table and chair
- A sign showing product and price
- A box with assorted change
- A plastic pitcher filled with lemonade

OLD-FASHIONED LEMONADE

1 cup sugar
1 cup fresh lemon juice (squeezed and
tasted—pucker up!—by the child)

5 cups water
Extra lemons slices (to float)

1. Mix together the first three
   ingredients.
2. Stir well to dissolve the sugar.

3. Add ice and garnish with
   lemon slices.

Loving, Long-Distance

A parent may not live close to her or his child. Frequent one-to-one encounters may not be possible. Likewise, in a country where well over half of grandparents live more than 300 miles away, it is no small feat to maintain a satisfying bond. For adults who want to make a difference in preschoolers' lives, here are a few time-honored ways to build loving links across the miles:

* Tape-record a reading of a requested picture book (jingling a small bell or making a similar sound at each turn of the page). Mail the book-and-tape set once a month or once a season.

(Or provide a taped reading of a library book; once the tape arrives, the caregiver can buy or borrow the same book.) The voice of an absent loved one enriches bedtime read-alouds. Once a preschooler knows how to operate a tape player, both story and beloved grown-up can be conjured up independently.

* Initiate an annual ritual. Pick out a Halloween pumpkin before sipping cider with doughnuts every October. Take in a garage sale or a concert in the park each summer. Make a yearly trip together to the church bazaar, to the St. Patrick's Day parade, to the zoo.

* Enjoy a five-minute phone call at the same time each week or month when grown-up and child converse only with each other about something that:
  1. They've each seen;
  2. The child did;
  3. Made one of them happy, scared, or surprised; or
  4. The grown-up values about the young listener.

* To mark the beginning or end of each visit, invariably walk to the local playground, the ice cream shop, the nearest woodland trail, or around the block.

* Periodically, welcome videos, photos, or e-mails, showing how the preschooler is growing. Reciprocate, letting the child see you in your setting, too.

* Store special finds in a keepsake box—a funny picture, a unique rock, a glitzy toy ring, a feather, a medal, or other little treasures to share on the next visit. Preschoolers can be motivated to start a box of their own for later showing and sharing.

Someone Special, Just Like You

by Tricia Brown, photographed by Fran Ortiz, with bibliography by Effie Lee Morris. New York: Holt, Rinehart and Winston, 1984.

THE AUTHOR OF THIS CLASSIC insists that this is not a book about children with disabilities, but about all of us, young and old alike, for "we all have our own disabilities in one way or another, and each of us is someone special." The black-and-white photographs that complement the simple text have a timeless quality, capturing children of varying abilities learning, achieving, and interacting with each other and with loving adults. Children with a range of abilities and traits exude a sense of optimism about life and themselves. Each feels of value. As the framework of Developmental Assets describes, they expect their presence and activities to gain positive responses from others.

Before You Read Together

If you ask what she notices, the child may comment that this cover is a photograph of real children, rather than an illustrated picture. Does he guess that the large wheel in the background belongs to a wheelchair? Does she know a friend with glasses? The word *special* in the title is likely to have positive connotations, and *just like you* indicates that the subject of the story and the listener have much in common. The photos of children doing the very things the child can do reinforce this impression. You might let her know that it's actually about all kinds of special people, not just one person as the word *someone* suggests.

After You Read Aloud

- Depending on the child's age, the first large picture or others may be taken in stride or elicit a comment or question, especially since the next page confirms that the child is "someone just like you." A child of 3 may take this statement at "face value," noting only skin color differences. By 4, a child will notice actual differences, from gender to age to eye shape, pointing them out. Acknowledge these. Note that each of us has different ways of looking and moving and doing, but that we also play and love and think in common ways. We all have feelings. Each of us feels hurt when someone laughs at us or teases us. Each of us wants to make friends, to be happy.

Different but the Same

It's important to share books that integrate children with disabilities into the story and illustration without lots of fanfare or focusing on the disability. Examples include *ABC for You and Me* by Meg Girnis (in which a boy with Down's Syndrome introduces the alphabet), *The Balancing Girl* by Berniece Rabe, and *No Fair to Tigers/No es justo para los tigres* by Eric Hoffman. The preschool set, however, benefits from more information.

Despite our emphasis on what we all share in common, a young child may feel nervous when face-to-face with someone who seems different. Preschoolers may worry that they, too, will somehow become unable to walk or see or hear. An encounter with a person who is "differently abled" can make them feel vulnerable, unsure. Laughter, while inappropriate, may serve to reduce their anxiety.

Young children's fears about people who are physically different from them are natural at this stage of development. Young children will be more relaxed and open if they are helped to face their fears as well as provided information about the disabilities. The bibliography in *Someone Special, Just Like You* or a librarian serve as a resource for books about specific disabilities.

Firsthand experience is the best teacher—exploring Grandpa's hearing aid, learning the alphabet or certain symbols in sign language, seeing how a wheelchair works, admiring a Seeing Eye dog and talking to its owner. If an adult avoids contact with a person who has a disability, if a child senses that she can't ask questions or appear to notice a difference, if a grown-up treats a disabled child in an unnatural way, the preschooler is much more likely to follow suit. He may fail to recognize the disabled child's strength, bravery, and resourceful adaptation to the world.

Clay! Hooray!

Sculptor and woodcarver David Frykman told me that as a small child he knew what he was going to be when he grew up. He was sick and heading by train to the Mayo Clinic in Rochester, Minnesota, with his mother when she pulled out a package of modeling clay to help him relax and pass the time. He vividly remembers the feel of the clay in his hands, the joy he felt molding it into animal shapes. He's been creating and carving whimsical animals and human figures ever since.

Most children love clay. And virtually anyone, regardless of abilities, can mold snakes and spheres and silly shapes into being. Splurge on the real deal—nontoxic artist's gray clay that dries hard in the air or in a kiln. You can honor people of all colors by using Colorations dough that comes in a range of skin tones for clay figures. Or, make your own clay, and let it be what it will be. (See "Resources" on page 224 for a source of Colorations dough.)

MODELING CLAY

2 cups salt

2/3 cup water

1 cup cornstarch

1/2 cup cold water

The adult should make this recipe because it involves a hot stove and hot liquids.

1. Stir salt and 2/3 cup water in a saucepan over medium heat for about five minutes.

2. Remove from heat. Mix in cornstarch and cold water, stirring until smooth.

3. Return to the stove and cook until clay thickens.

4. Remove from the pan and allow to cool. Soak pan in water immediately to prevent the clay from hardening onto the sides or bottom.

5. Mold the cooled clay into desired shapes.

6. When the clay becomes hard, you and the preschooler can decorate it with paints. Store any leftover clay in a plastic bag for future use.

Famous Friendships

Nothing makes our differences seem so beside the point as friendship. Now the preschooler is actively engaged in learning the ropes—trusting that she is likable, compromising in order to play with others, figuring out this business of sharing and showing respect for another's rights and feelings. Fortunately, there are many classic stories about buddies to help children as they begin the process of finding a few irreplaceable friends of their own. Some famous friends worth knowing appear in the following picture books:

The Adventures of Sugar and Junior by Angela Shelf Medearis

Amos and Boris by William Steig

Be Quiet, Marina! by Kirsten DeBear

Benjamin and Tulip by Rosemary Wells

Big Al by Andrew Clements

Bill and Pete by Tomie dePaola

Frog and Toad All Year by Arnold Lobel (and others in the series)

George and Martha by James Marshall (and others in the series)

Lottie's New Friend by Petra Mathers (and others in the series)

Margaret and Margarita/Margarita y Margaret by Lynn Reiser

Toot and Puddle by Holly Hobbie (and others in the series)

Yo? Yes! by Chris Raschka

I Like Me!

by Nancy Carlson. New York: Viking Penguin, 1990.

AN OUTGOING PIG ON THE COVER puts her best foot forward, admitting at the outset: "I have a best friend. That best friend is me." Celebrating a range of "fun things" she can do and ways she takes care of herself, she highlights personal features of which she's especially fond—her curly tail, her round tummy, and her tiny little feet—and exudes plenty of self-confidence. She admits that sometimes she feels bad or makes mistakes, but that she picks herself up and is willing to "try and try again." Since pigs tend to get a bad rap, an unlikely heroine and the comical illustrations make this feel-good fiction for kids who can count the ways they are likable and capable, too.

Before You Read Together

Here's one happy pig in a polka-dot dress, with front hooves raised in triumph beneath the title that says it all: I LIKE ME! Point out the exclamation mark (!), explaining that this punctuation mark tells readers to say words loudly, in excitement or in a shout. You may want to explore if any pigs in the real world dress up—emphasizing the silliness that lies ahead. Both of you can shout out "I like me," making it more likely that the child will compare the pig's reasons with his own.

After You Read Aloud

- Folding several sheets of paper in half, you can make a book that mimics this one. Put a picture of the child on the cover or invite her to draw a self-portrait. In large letters, print the words *I LIKE ME!* overhead. Ask the preschooler to supply reasons why she likes herself: What is she proud that she can do? In what ways does she have fun? How does she take care of herself? How has she helped or cheered up another? Depending on the child's age and ability, have her draw pictures to illustrate the comments or help by sketching something or cutting out a magazine picture to represent her reason (e.g., a toothbrush if she's proud of brushing her teeth). Encourage her to show or "read" her book to family members and grown-up friends.

Pass the Praise, Please

Some forms of praise should be kept out of the reach of small children (see "Negative Praise" on the next page). That said, bring on generous helpings of encouragement in the form of hugs, applause, smiles, kind words, and your mindful presence. The daily doses of positive feedback that researchers have found to be so instrumental in preschoolers' future success are spontaneous and nonjudgmental. Express confidence and trust in each and every child by serving up phrases like these:

* "Yes! You did it! I just knew you could!"
* "I see you brushed your teeth really well. You're getting better and better at it."
* "What an interesting idea!" Or "I'm glad you shared your feelings. I hear you."
* "Everybody makes mistakes. I see you're willing to try again."
* "I love dancing with you." Or "I'm so thankful you're in the world." Or "Your smile brightens my day."

For *kids are worth it!* author Barbara Coloroso, encouraging a child means sending "the six critical life messages":

1. I believe in you.
2. I trust you.
3. I know you can handle this.
4. You are listened to.
5. You are cared for.
6. You are very important to me.

Post the six messages as reminders on the fridge or the classroom wall. The resilient child—who can say with confidence, "I like me!"—is one who regularly receives these messages from loving grown-ups in their words and in their actions.

I See You

Whenever a child had to move away during the school year, the class and I sat in a circle to give a gift to the one who was leaving. The departing student chose a small stone from a tray and it moved from hand to hand, taking in the energy of every person. As each of us held it, we offered a positive comment about the person who was leaving.

I remember one such ceremony, in particular. The news of this child's imminent departure had been a source of relief for more than one in the class. He'd acted troubled and, in relation to others, troublesome a number of times. There were obviously negative comments or old grudges that could be aired, but the children rose to the occasion. As one after another expressed something they valued about this boy, and, at times, added a wish for his well-being in a new setting, the effect on everybody was transforming.

The givers of honest affirmations saw and honored the whole person and the receiver sat, stunned, by the expressed good will, the reminders, which he would take with him, that he had value. It was such a meaningful ceremony that I began devoting the last week of every school year to letting every child, in turn, be beneficiary of the small stone, a talisman to carry into the world, along with the affirming words from peers and me.

My friend Karen, an early childhood educator, told me of a similar ritual that she has enjoyed with preschoolers. On birthdays, around a table they pass a saucer to which a small lighted votive candle is securely glued in the center. As the candle appears before a child, each takes a moment to tell something he or she likes about the birthday boy or girl who, at the end, gets to blow out the candle.

NEGATIVE PRAISE

Some forms of praise create "approval addicts" or "praise junkies," says author Barbara Coloroso, author of *kids are worth it!* Avoid these kinds:

* Compliments offered for an ulterior motive: "You're such a good sister that I know you can watch the baby while I do the laundry."
* Comments that pit a child against a sibling or friend: "If only your brother was as good about putting away his toys." "Wow! You're better than anyone else in the class."
* Conditional praise that only comes if one works for it: "Since you behaved in the mall, I'll buy you a toy."
* Dishonest praise that makes it risky to make mistakes: "You're the best artist I've ever known."

If such distinctions confuse you, take a look at her book. She shows why children cannot thrive on bribes, threats, rewards, or punishment, whether doled out in or out of the home.

Each of these rituals says: "You are known and valued. I see you. You are not invisible." These are important messages to hear and take to heart, regardless of one's age or stage of development.

True Calling

Perhaps the young child you know and love has a surprising talent or interest. Researchers and caregivers alike puzzle over what many young children bring to life so early in their years. Biographies abound with real-life examples of people who recognized, as very young children, what it was they loved. Looking back, each admits that even at 4 or 5, they had talent, vision, or commitment that helped them to become what they were meant to be. And often they had someone to encourage them, to make it possible to follow where their interest would lead.

So much conspires to keep us from being true to ourselves. Young children need people in their lives to witness quietly to what ignites the spirit and then to give them their blessing. My friend Diana remembers that "fuff" (for *flower*) was the very first word uttered by her son, now an environmentalist. She witnessed and celebrated his choices from an early age.

Observe what truly engages a child. Listen and honor her impressions. Show appreciation for his novel ideas. Provide opportunities for learning and play that the child initiates. In a folder, collect clippings about topics and coming events that seem especially suited to this preschooler.

A child may find himself in a family that does not honor or accept his way of being. Instead the grown-ups' unspoken messages are: "Do what I love to do." "Prize what the rest of us value." "Follow *my* agenda." Psychologist Tobin Hart, in *The Secret Spiritual World of Children*, writes: "We nourish the child's integrity when our messages both spoken and silent are, 'You don't have to be anyone but who you are . . .'"

Read the classic about a young gardener, *The Carrot Seed*, by Ruth Krauss. Perhaps it's a favorite story with the youngest because in the face of all the naysayers who repeatedly tell a small boy that nothing will come of his efforts to grow a carrot, he triumphs in the end. Realizing his vision—after following his passion—he hauls away an amazing specimen. It's a source of wonder. Wonder-filled books brim with possibility. In so many jaw-dropping ways, so do young children.

Positive-Identity Bonus Best Bets

- **Big Brother Dustin** by R. Carter Alden, photographed by Dan Young with Carol Carter. Cambridge, MA: Candlewick Press, 2001.

- **Black is brown is tan** by Arnold Adoff, illustrated by Emily Arnold McCully. New York: HarperCollins, 2002.

- **Catherine and Laurence Anholt's Big Book of Little Children** by Catherine and Laurence Anholt. Cambridge, MA: Candlewick Press, 2003.

- **Cleversticks** by Bernard Ashley, illustrated by Derek Brazell. New York: Crown, 1992.

- **Ella Sarah Gets Dressed** by Margaret Chodos-Irvine. San Diego: Harcourt, 2003.

- **Two Homes** by Claire Masurel, illustrated by Kady MacDonald Denton. Cambridge, MA: Candlewick Press, 2001.

- **Without Words** by Joanne Ryder, with photographs by Barbara Sonneborn. San Francisco: Sierra Club Books for Children, 1995.

Epilogue

· ·

In *The World According to Mister Rogers*, a collection of quotations of the late, great friend of young children everywhere, the dedication page reads: "To anyone who has loved you into being . . ."

What a concept! Parents, of course, are the ones who usher a human being into the world, and it's the fortunate child who is welcomed by them with joy and nurtured with loving care through childhood and beyond. However, parents have no monopoly on loving. And rarely can they alone provide all that's required.

Certainly, in our being and becoming, love is what matters. As you grew, which individuals—offering attention and affection—loved you into being, into becoming the person you are today? For what child or group of children are you now doing likewise?

Behind every Developmental Asset is loving attention. It shapes the efforts of caregivers and educators and relatives and neighbors. It inspires community action. Anyone can bring this gift, in varied ways, to bear on a life. Isn't that the point of all these rituals, everyday recipes and activities, mindful reflections, and animated engagement?

We dare not underestimate the power that resides in simply reading aloud a book and then another, in entering into children's play and into their hearts. It's in these ways, linking literacy and asset building, that we will raise a generation of readers and leaders. In these ways, one child at a time, we can transform the world.

Appendixes

Prototype Early Childhood Developmental Assets Framework

External Assets

Support

1. **Family support**—Primary caregivers, at least one of whom is a member of the child's immediate family, consistently and predictably provide high levels of love, physical care, attention, and nurturing in a way responsive to the child's individuality.
2. **Positive family communication**—Primary caregivers communicate positively, openly, and respectfully, expressing themselves in a language and style appropriate to children's age, developmental level, and individuality.
3. **Other adult relationships**—With the support of their family, children experience interactions and relationships with non-familial adults, including caregivers, relatives, older people, and community figures. These interactions are characterized by investment, enrichment, consistency, and caring.
4. **Caring neighbors**—Young children know neighbors that extend both the child's network of relationships and sense of safety and protection.
5. **Caring alternative care and school climate**—Alternative caregivers and teachers, whether within or outside of the home, are nurturing and accepting, and provide stability and security.
6. **Parent involvement in early care and education**—Parents, teachers, and caregivers communicate with each other in order to attain a consistent and understanding approach to young children. Parents play various roles in the child-care and educational setting.

Empowerment

7. Community cherishes and values young children—
Communities are responsive to issues relevant to the well-being
of young children, offering an array of activities and quality
resources, including those that promote physical health, appropriate to their developmental characteristics and needs.

8. Young children receive and are seen as resources—
Communities show their caring and investment in young children's futures through community system building and by providing families what they need to function as a "child rearing
system" and providing alternative caregivers and child-care
programs with adequate financial subsidy.

9. Young children are able to make a contribution—Young
children are provided opportunities to offer assistance and help
with simple chores that bring pleasure and order to their environment, and enable them to feel valued.

10. Young children feel and are safe—Adults, including parents,
caregivers, and neighbors, are able to reassure young children
that their safety and well-being are a high priority, and that
they are protected. The community provides physical safety,
opportunity for physical development, and access to adequate
health care.

Boundaries and Expectations

11. Family boundaries—The family makes reasonable, developmentally appropriate guidelines for acceptable behavior by
young children in ways that are understandable and attainable
by young children.

12. Alternative care or out-of-home boundaries—Alternative
care and early education programs use positive ways of implic-
itly and explicitly teaching young children acceptable behavior;
they avoid inappropriate and punitive methods that confuse,
shame, and isolate.

13. Neighborhood boundaries—Neighbors encourage positive
and acceptable behavior in young children in a supportive, non-
threatening way.

14. **Adult role models**—Adults serve as role models by showing the same kind of self-regulation, empathy, acceptance of others, and engagement with learning that they would expect and value in young children.

15. **Positive peer relationships**—Young children's peers offer inclusion and acceptance, opportunity for having fun in constructive play, and opportunity for developing and practicing prosocial skills.

16. **Positive expectations**—Adults expect young children to behave appropriately, undertake challenging tasks with their assistance, and to do well at an activity within the child's capacity to perform by giving encouragement. They avoid negative labeling if the child does not succeed.

Constructive Use of Time

17. **Play and creative activities**—Young children have daily opportunities to play with a variety of developmentally appropriate materials, both structured and unstructured, that allow self-expression, physical activity, and interaction with others.

18. **Out-of-home and community programs**—Young children are exposed to developmentally appropriate out-of-home programs staffed with competent adults that offer a variety of well-maintained, suitable materials. Children are periodically taken to community settings such as parks, museums, and theaters that offer stimulating experiences.

19. **Religious experiences**—Young children participate in age-appropriate spiritual activities that reflect the family's faith and beliefs, such as the role of faith in building feelings of security, optimism, and caring for others, and that address their own emerging interest in religious issues.

20. **Time at home**—Young children spend a major portion of their time at home where they receive individual attention from primary caregivers, participate in family activities, play with a variety of materials, interact with nonfamily visitors of all ages, and view TV minimally.

Internal Assets

Commitment to Learning

21. **Motivation to mastery**—Young children respond to novelty and new experiences with interest, curiosity, and energy reflective of physical well-being, leading to successful and pleasurable experiences.

22. **Active participation in learning experiences**—Young children are engaged and invested in developmentally appropriate materials and experiences.

23. **Bonding to alternative care programs**—Young children feel positive about their ongoing attendance in out-of-home care and educational programs, and after an initial period of adjustment, attend willingly.

24. **Home-school connection**—Young children experience security, connection, and consistency between home and school or other out-of-home programs as a result of mutual concern by adults at each site, and through sharing information about concerns, interests, and activities.

25. **Early literacy**—Young children increasingly show interest in print material and representational symbols (pictures, letters, numbers) as a result of being involved in language-rich activities, particularly being read to frequently and being exposed to print materials.

Positive Values

26. **Caring**—Young children begin showing empathy, understanding, and awareness of others' feelings, and make comforting and accepting gestures to peers and others in distress.

27. **Equality and social justice**—Young children show concern for people who are at a disadvantage or who are excluded from activities because they are different.

28. **Integrity**—Young children express their worldviews in various ways, which include asking questions, making comments, and enacting play episodes. They are also increasingly able to stand up for their own sense of justice.

29. **Honesty**—Young children come to understand the prosocial value of honesty and are truthful to the extent their construction of and perception of reality permits.

30. **Responsibility**—Young children can carry out or follow through on simple tasks that help or benefit others.

Social Competencies

31. **Interpersonal skills**—Young children have "friendship skills." They can play harmoniously with their peers through cooperation, give and take of ideas, and increasing ability to share, and by showing interest in and awareness of the feelings of others.

32. **Self-regulation**—Young children increasingly can identify the emotions they are feeling, are able to regulate their emotions in conflictual and stressful situations, and can focus their attention when needed on a matter at hand.

33. **Planning and problem solving**—Young children can intentionally plan for the immediate future, make a choice among several options, and attempt to solve problems or surmount frustrations.

34. **Cultural awareness and sensitivity**—Young children show positive and accepting attitudes toward people who are racially, physically, culturally, or ethnically different from themselves.

35. **Resistance skills**—Young children have an increasingly accurate sense of danger appropriate to their expanding sense of self and environmental knowledge, seek protective help from trusted adults, and resist pressure from peers to participate in unacceptable behavior.

36. **Conflict resolution**—Young children are increasingly able to mediate harmonious responses to conflicts by being helped to see the other person's perspective and learning how to compromise in a mutually respectful way.

Positive Identity

37. **Personal power**—Young children have a sense of being able to make something happen that matters to them and to others.

38. **Positive self-esteem**—Young children have a growing sense that they are valued and that their presence and activities gain positive responses from others.

39. **Positive view of personal future**—Young children feel a sense of optimism—that life is exciting and enjoyable, and that they have a positive place within it.

40. **Sense of purpose**—Young children look forward to appropriate milestones that will energize and confirm their growth, such as upcoming birthdays, holidays, kindergarten, and school entrance.

Library List
of Featured Books

Support

- **Molly Goes Shopping** by Eva Eriksson, translated by Elisabeth Kallick Dyssegaard. New York: R & S Books, 2003.

- **A Birthday for Frances** by Russell Hoban, illustrated by Lillian Hoban. New York: HarperCollins, 1995.

- **Adam's Daycare** by Julie Ovenell-Carter, illustrated by Ruth Ohi. Toronto: Annick Press, 1997.

- **Somebody Loves You, Mr. Hatch** by Eileen Spinelli, illustrated by Paul Yalowitz. New York: Simon & Schuster, 1991.

- **The Key to My Heart** by Nira Harel, illustrated by Yossi Abulafia. La Jolla, CA: Kane/Miller, 2003.

Empowerment

- **Edward in Deep Water** by Rosemary Wells. New York: Dial Books for Young Readers, 1995.

- **Flower Garden** by Eve Bunting, illustrated by Kathryn Hewitt. San Diego: Voyager Books/Harcourt, 2000.

- **Queenie, One of the Family** by Bob Graham. Cambridge, MA: Candlewick Press, 1997.

- **You Can Do It, Sam** by Amy Hest, illustrated by Anita Jeram. Cambridge, MA: Candlewick Press, 2003.

- **Piggy Washes Up** by Carol Thompson. Cambridge, MA: Candlewick Press, 1989 (U.S. edition 1997).

Boundaries & Expectations

- **How Do Dinosaurs Say Goodnight?** by Jane Yolen, illustrated by Mark Teague. New York: The Blue Sky Press/Scholastic, 2000. (Spanish edition: *¿Cómo dan las buenas noches los dinosaurios?*)

- **Now I'm Big** by Margaret Miller. New York: Greenwillow Books, 1996.

- **Don't Let the Pigeon Drive the Bus!** by Mo Willems. New York: Hyperion Books for Children, 2003.

- **Trashy Town** by Andrea Zimmerman and David Clemesha, illustrated by Dan Yaccarino. New York: HarperCollins, 1999.

- **Officer Buckle and Gloria** by Peggy Rathmann. New York: G. P. Putnam's Sons, 1995.

Constructive Use of Time

- **Owl Moon** by Jane Yolen, illustrated by John Schoenherr. New York: Philomel Books, 1987.

- **Jingle Dancer** by Cynthia Leitich Smith, illustrated by Cornelius Van Wright and Ying-Hwa Hu. New York: Morrow Junior Books, 2000.

- **A Child's Calendar** by John Updike, illustrated by Trina Schart Hyman. New York: Holiday House, 1999.

- **Hurray for Pre-K!** by Ellen B. Senisi. New York: HarperCollins, 2000.

- **In Every Tiny Grain of Sand: A Child's Book of Prayers and Praise** by Reeve Lindbergh, illustrated by Christine Davenier, Bob Graham, Anita Jeram, and Elisa Kleven. Cambridge, MA: Candlewick Press, 2000.

Commitment to Learning

- **Wemberly Worried** by Kevin Henkes. New York: Greenwillow Books/HarperCollins, 2000.

- **And If the Moon Could Talk** by Kate Banks, illustrated by Georg Hallensleben. New York: Frances Foster Books/Farrar, Straus & Giroux, 1998.

- **Where Did You Get Your Moccasins?** by Bernelda Wheeler, illustrated by Herman Bekkering. Winnipeg, Canada: Peguis, 1992.

- **Toot & Puddle: Puddle's ABC** by Holly Hobbie. Boston: Little, Brown, 2000.

- **The Jamie and Angus Stories** by Anne Fine, illustrated by Penny Dale. Cambridge, MA: Candlewick Press, 2002.

Positive Values

- **Stella, Queen of the Snow** by Marie-Louise Gay. Toronto: Groundwood/Douglas & McIntyre, 2000.

- **Jamela's Dress** by Niki Daly. New York: Farrar, Straus & Giroux, 1999.

- **The Tomten** by Astrid Lindgren. New York: Puffin, 1997.

- **All about Alfie** by Shirley Hughes. New York: Lothrop, Lee & Shepard Books/Morrow Junior Books, 1997.

- **The Empty Pot** by Demi. New York: Henry Holt, 1990.

Social Competencies

- **Each Living Thing** by Joanne Ryder, illustrated by Ashley Wolff. San Diego: Gulliver Books/Harcourt, 2000.

- **Bein' with You This Way** by W. Nikola-Lisa, illustrated by Michael Bryant. New York: Lee & Low Books, 1994.

- **The Ugly Vegetables** by Grace Lin. Watertown, MA: Talewinds/Charlesbridge, 1999.

- **This Is Our House** by Michael Rosen, illustrated by Bob Graham. Cambridge, MA: Candlewick Press, 1996.

- **When Sophie Gets Angry—Really, Really Angry . . .** by Molly Bang. New York: The Blue Sky Press/Scholastic, 1999. (Spanish edition: **Cuando Sofía se enoja, se enoja de veras . . .**)

Positive Identity

- **Con Mi Hermano/With My Brother** por/by Eileen Roe, ilustraciones por/illustrations by Robert Casilla. New York: Simon & Schuster Books for Young Readers/Aladdin Paperbacks, 1994.

- **The First Thing My Mama Told Me** by Susan Marie Swanson, illustrated by Christine Davenier. San Diego: Harcourt, 2002.

- **Taxi! Taxi!** by Cari Best, illustrated by Dale Gottlieb. New York: Orchard Books, 1997.

- **Someone Special, Just Like You** by Tricia Brown, photographed by Fran Ortiz, with bibliography by Effie Lee Morris. New York: Holt, Rinehart and Winston, 1984.

- **I Like Me!** by Nancy Carlson. New York: Viking Penguin, 1990.

Bonus Library List of Books

Support

- **dear juno** by Soyung Pak, illustrated by Susan Kathleen Hartung. New York: Viking, 1999.

- **It Takes a Village** by Jane Cowan-Fletcher. New York: Scholastic Press, 1994.

- **Lilly's Purple Plastic Purse** by Kevin Henkes. New York: Greenwillow Books, 1996.

- **Old MacDonald** by Amy Schwartz. New York: Scholastic Press, 1999.

- **On Mother's Lap** by Ann Herbert Scott, illustrated by Glo Coalson. New York: McGraw-Hill, 1972.

- **The Sick Day** by Patricia MacLachlan, illustrated by Jane Dyer. New York: Random House Children's Books, 2001.

- **The Story of Little Babaji** by Helen Bannerman, illustrated by Fred Marcellino. New York: HarperCollins, 1996.

Empowerment

- **All by Myself!** by Aliki. New York: HarperCollins, 2000.

- **Can I Help?** by Marilyn Janovitz. New York: North-South Books, 1996.

- **Good Dog, Paw!** by Chinlun Lee. Cambridge, MA: Candlewick Press, 2004.

- **I Can't Talk Yet but When I Do . . .** by Julie Markes, illustrated by Laura Rader. New York: HarperCollins, 2003.

- **Mole and the Baby Bird** by Marjorie Newman, illustrated by Patrick Benson. New York: Bloomsbury Children's Books, 2002.

- **My Mama Sings** by Jeanne Whitehouse Peterson, illustrated by Sandra Speidel. New York: HarperCollins, 1994.

- **Wilfrid Gordon McDonald Partridge** by Mem Fox. Brooklyn, NY: Kane/Miller, 1996.

Boundaries & Expectations

- **D. W. the Picky Eater** by Marc Brown. Boston: Little, Brown, 1995.

- **Fireman Small** by Wong Herbert Yee. Boston: Houghton Mifflin, 1994.

- **Harriet, You'll Drive Me Wild!** by Mem Fox. San Diego: Harcourt, 2000.

- **The Runaway Bunny** by Margaret Wise Brown. New York: HarperFestival, 2001 (oversize board book edition).

- **The Tale of Peter Rabbit** by Beatrix Potter. London: Frederick Warne, 1902, 1987 (original and authorized edition).

- **Voyage to the Bunny Planet (First Tomato, Moss Pillows, and The Island Light)** by Rosemary Wells. New York: Dial Books for Young Readers, 1992.

- **We Can Do It!** by Laura Dwight. New York: Star Bright Books, 1997.

Constructive Use of Time

- **Father Fox's Pennyrhymes** by Clyde Watson, illustrated by Wendy Watson. New York: HarperCollins, 2001.

- **Max Found Two Sticks** by J. Brian Pinkney. New York: Simon & Schuster Books for Young Readers, 1994.

- **Peter Spier's Rain** by Peter Spier. Garden City, NY: Bantam Doubleday Dell Books for Young Readers, 1997.

- **Pretend You're a Cat** by Jean Marzollo, illustrated by Jerry Pinkney. New York: Puffin Pied Piper/Penguin, 1997.

- **Stella and Roy Go Camping** by Ashley Wolff. New York: Dutton Children's Books, 1999.

- **A Summery Saturday Morning** by Margaret Mahy. New York: Viking, 1998.

- **Sunday** by Synthia Saint James. Morton Grove, IL: Albert Whitman, 1996.

Commitment to Learning

- **Alfie's ABC** by Shirley Hughes. New York: Lothrop, Lee & Shepard Books, 1998.

- **At School: A Lift-the-Flap Learning Book** by Francisco Pittau and Bernadette Gervais. Éditions du Seuil: San Francisco Chronicle Books, 2003.

- **Curious Kids Go to Preschool: Another Big Book of Words** by Heloise Antoine, illustrated by Ingrid Godon. Atlanta, GA: Peachtree, 1996.

- **First Day** by Dandi Daley Mackall. San Diego: Harcourt, 2003.

- **Harry and the Bucketful of Dinosaurs** by Ian Whybrow, illustrated by Adrian Reynolds. New York: Random House, 2003. (Previously published as *Sammy and the Dinosaurs*. New York: Orchard Books, 1999).

- **Talking Like the Rain** selected by X. J. and Dorothy Kennedy. Boston: Little, Brown, 1992.

- **Usborne First 100 Words in Spanish** by Heather Amery, illustrated by Stephen Cartwright, with translation and pronunciation guide by Jane Straker. London: Usborne, 2002 (U.S. edition).

Positive Values

- **Arnie and the Stolen Markers** by Nancy Carlson. New York: Viking Kestral, 1987.

- **Building a Bridge** by Lisa Shook Begay. Flagstaff, AZ: Rising Moon/Northland, 1993.

- **Dogger** by Shirley Hughes. New York: Lothrop, Lee & Shepard Books, 1988.

- **The Lady and the Spider** by Faith McNulty, illustrated by Bob Marstall. New York: HarperCollins, 1987.

- **A Song for Lena** by Hilary Horder Hippely. New York: Simon & Schuster Books for Young Readers, 1996.

- **10 Minutes till Bedtime** by Peggy Rathmann. New York: Puffin, 2004.

- **Visiting Day** by Jacqueline Woodson, illustrated by James E. Ransome. New York: Scholastic Press, 2002.

Social Competencies

- **And to Think That We Thought That We'd Never Be Friends** by Mary Ann Hoberman, illustrated by Kevin Hawkes. New York: Crown, 1999.

- **The Colors of Us** by Karen Katz. New York: Henry Holt, 1999.

- **Goodbye Mousie** by Robie H. Harris, illustrated by Jan Ormerod. New York: Margaret K. McElderry Books, 2001.

- **Margaret and Margarita/Margarita y Margaret** by Lynn Reiser. New York: Greenwillow, 1993.

- **¡Pío Peep! Traditional Spanish Nursery Rhymes** selected by Alma Flor Ada and F. Isabel Campoy, translated by Alice Schertle and illustrated by Viví Escrivá. New York: HarperCollins, 2003.

- **Stone Soup** by Jon J. Muth. New York: Scholastic Press, 2003.

- **Whoever You Are** by Mem Fox. San Diego: Voyager/Harcourt, 1997.

Positive Identity

- **Big Brother Dustin** by R. Carter Alden, photographed by Dan Young with Carol Carter. Cambridge, MA: Candlewick Press, 2001.

- **Black is brown is tan** by Arnold Adoff, illustrated by Emily Arnold McCully. New York: HarperCollins, 2002.

- **Catherine and Laurence Anholt's Big Book of Little Children** by Catherine and Laurence Anholt. Cambridge, MA: Candlewick Press, 2003.

- **Cleversticks** by Bernard Ashley, illustrated by Derek Brazell. New York: Crown, 1992.

- **Ella Sarah Gets Dressed** by Margaret Chodos-Irvine. San Diego: Harcourt, 2003.

- **Two Homes** by Claire Masurel, illustrated by Kady MacDonald Denton. Cambridge, MA: Candlewick Press, 2001.

- **Without Words** by Joanne Ryder, with photographs by Barbara Sonneborn. San Francisco: Sierra Club Books for Children, 1995.

Is Your Child Ready to Read?

• •

The child who is ready to read:

* Knows alphabet letters are a special type of graphic that can be recognized individually;
* Knows that it is units of print that are read and read aloud in books;
* Identifies at least 10 alphabet letters, especially those in one's own name;
* Shows interest in books and listens carefully;
* Attends to beginning, repeating and rhyming sounds in words;
* Uses new words and longer sentences when speaking and pretending to read;
* Understands that different texts (recipes, brochures, street signs) are used for different purposes;
* Writes (scribbles) messages as part of playful and pretend activities;
* Recognizes familiar print, such as signs in the classroom or on the road;
* Understands and follows spoken directions; and
* Asks questions, makes comments, and understands the book being read aloud.

Sources: *A Child Becomes a Reader: Birth through Preschool* by Bonnie B. Armbuster, Ph.D., Fran Lehr, M.A., and Jean Osborn, M.Ed. Portsmouth, NH: RMC Research Corp., 2003. (Free copy available from The National Institute for Literacy at: edpuborders@edpubs.org.) Also: *The Early Bird Project Handbook* by Carolyn (Tunie) Munson-Benson. Minnetonka, MN: 2002.

Resources

Acknowledgments

. . . .

Book Credits

Pages 15, 193	*Touchpoints Three to Six: Your Child's Emotional and Behavioral Development* by T. Berry Brazelton, M.D., and Joshua D. Sparrow, M.D. Copyright © 2001. Perseus Publishing. Cambridge, MA.
Pages 28, 64	From *Meaningful Differences in the Everyday Experience of Young American Children* by Betty Hart and Todd R. Risley. Copyright © 1995 by Paul H. Brookes Publishing Company, Inc., Baltimore, MD.
Page 50	Activity on page 551, "Washing Hands" (a.k.a. "Soap Wins, Hands Down"), from *GIANT Encyclopedia of Preschool Activities for Three-Year-Olds,* (ISBN 0-87659-237-X), formerly titled "It's Great to be Three" by Kathy Charner, are reprinted with permission from Gryphon House, P.O. Box 207, Beltsville, MD 20704-0207. (800) 638-0928.
Pages 66, 202, 203	Text as submitted from *kids are worth it!* by Barbara Coloroso. Copyright © 1994 by Barbara Coloroso. Reprinted by permission of HarperCollins Publishers, Inc. Also from *kids are worth it!* by Barbara Coloroso. Copyright © Barbara Coloroso, 2000. Reprinted by permission of Penguin Group (Canada).
Page 74	"Pretzels" activity from *Teaching Children to Care* by Ruth Sidney Charney. Copyright © 2002 by Northeast Foundation for Children. Appears by permission of Northeast Foundation for Children, Turners Falls, MA.

Cover Illustration Credits

Page 1   *The Key to My Heart* by Nira Harel, copyright © 2003. Reproduced by permission of the publisher, Kane/Miller Book Publishers, La Jolla, CA.

Page 27   Book cover from *Flower Garden,* text copyright © 1994 by Eve Bunting, illustrations copyright © 1994 by Kathryn Hewitt, reprinted by permission of Harcourt, Inc.

Page 55   *Officer Buckle and Gloria.* Text and illustrations copyright © 1996 by Peggy Rathmann. Published by G.P. Putnam's Sons, a member of Penguin Group (USA) Inc.

Page 79   *Owl Moon.* Text copyright © 1987 by Jane Yolen. Illlustrations copyright © 1987 by John Schoenherr. Published by Philomel Books, a member of Penguin Group (USA) Inc.

Page 103   *The Jamie and Angus Stories.* Text Copyright © 2002 Anne Fine; Illustrations Copyright © 2002 Penny Dale. Reproduced by permission of the publisher Candlewick Press, Inc., Cambridge, MA., on behalf of Walker Books Ltd., London.

Page 129   *The Empty Pot* by Demi, copyright © 1990. Reproduced by permission of the publisher Henry Holt and Company, LLC, New York, NY.

Page 155   Book cover from *Each Living Thing*, text copyright © 2000 by Ashley Wolff, reprinted by permission of Harcourt, Inc.

Page 181   *I Like Me.* Copyright © 1988 Nancy Carlson. Published by Viking Penguin Inc., a member of Penguin Group (USA) Inc.

Recipe Credits

Thanks to each of the following cooks for providing a recipe:
Susan Boulding, Ruby Duffield, Gudrun Milbrodt, Iola Schomburg, and Linda Tacke.

Additional Early Literacy Resources

- *Starting Out Right: A Guide to Promoting Children's Reading Success* by editors M. Susan Burns, Peg Griffin, and Catherine E. Snow. Washington, D.C.: National Academy Press, 1998.

- *Straight Talk about Reading: How Parents Can Make a Difference during the Early Years* by Susan J. Hall and Louisa C. Moats. Chicago: NTC Publishing Group, 1998

- *Much More Than the ABCs: The Early Stages of Reading and Writing* by Judith A. Schickendanz. Washington, D.C.: National Association for the Education of Young Children, 1999.